T0148059

SHE WAS ...
GOD'S JOYOUS MESSENGER

A Mother's Story of Love and Loss

KATHY SCHUSTER

Copyright © 2020 Kathy Schuster.

All rights reserved. No part of this book may be used or reproduced by
any means, graphic, electronic, or mechanical, including photocopying,
recording, taping or by any information storage retrieval system
without the written permission of the author except in the case of
brief quotations embodied in critical articles and reviews.

This book is a work of non-fiction. Unless otherwise noted, the author
and the publisher make no explicit guarantees as to the accuracy of
the information contained in this book and in some cases, names of
people and places have been altered to protect their privacy.

Archway Publishing books may be ordered through booksellers or by contacting:

Archway Publishing
1663 Liberty Drive
Bloomington, IN 47403
www.archwaypublishing.com
1 (888) 242-5904

Because of the dynamic nature of the Internet, any web addresses or
links contained in this book may have changed since publication and
may no longer be valid. The views expressed in this work are solely those
of the author and do not necessarily reflect the views of the publisher,
and the publisher hereby disclaims any responsibility for them.

Any people depicted in stock imagery provided by Getty Images are
models, and such images are being used for illustrative purposes only.
Certain stock imagery © Getty Images.

Cover/Interior Image Credit: Frank Nichols

THE HOLY BIBLE, NEW INTERNATIONAL VERSION®,
NIV® Copyright © 1973, 1978, 1984, 2011 by Biblica, Inc.®
Used by permission. All rights reserved worldwide.

ISBN: 978-1-4808-8580-6 (sc)
ISBN: 978-1-4808-8581-3 (e)

Library of Congress Control Number: 2019920122

Print information available on the last page.

Archway Publishing rev. date: 12/13/2019

This book is dedicated to the memory of my daughter, Angela. I could not have loved her more. She was God's joyous messenger to me and one of the greatest gifts I have ever been given. Along with her siblings Joshua, Bryan and Rebecca, Angela filled my life with joy and love as the blessed mother that I am. I thank God for my children and for my husband, Gordon, who has encouraged me to share my feelings and the loss of our daughter in this book.

Angela Joyce Schuster Svendsen

Contents

Acknowledgments

I would like to gratefully acknowledge the amazing people whose contributions provided invaluable assistance in preparing this manuscript. Thank you to Dale Bachman, who willingly and patiently helped me with my first draft. It was a bit scary to reveal the words taken from my heart and placed on paper to someone else. Your kindness and expertise were greatly appreciated and your meticulous editing allowed my "project" to become a reality. Thank you to Becky Bren and Susan Reed, both dear friends, who agreed to read through my manuscript early-on, and give me their personal opinions as to whether I had met my goals in writing it. Your observations and list of questions to be considered compelled me to write more specifically to my audience. I am so grateful for your influence. Thank you to Patsy Mugg, for assisting me so effortlessly with the pictures. I so appreciated your help. A special thank you to my sisters, Karen McArdel and Jennifer Gregg, for taking the time and emotional energy to read about our past lives as you perused my story. Thank you for allowing me to tell it just as I wrote it. And finally, I want to give a very heartfelt thanks, to my husband, Gordon, daughter, Rebecca, and sons, Joshua and Bryan, for your support and encouragement. Your editorial help and suggestions were the ones I valued most. One thing is for certain, without the input from you, my family, and those mentioned above, this book would probably never have been written.

Introduction

Grief will always be a part of the human experience on earth. No one can escape its painful grasp for very long. Though grief is universal it remains a very personal and unique journey to everyone who encounters it. This book is about my own personal grief story. My hope is that it will help others who are living in theirs.

Angela was my first-born child. She was a delightful little girl who grew into an accomplished young woman. Nothing could have prepared me for losing her, yet nothing in my life has changed me more than the grief I have grown through because of her death. I felt pain and I felt completely lost. At points I was not sure how I was going to live without her. Losing Angela changed every aspect of my life. I had no idea at the time of her death that the grief I felt was also connected to the losses I had endured as a teenager. I lost three family members within a three year period. This unprocessed layered grief, compounded with the death of my daughter, was extremely difficult to get through. God guided me as I looked back to my youth in order to move forward and grow through my present grief.

Prior to losing my daughter, I was confident that God was fully in control of my life, and the lives of my family members. Losing Angela tested my faith and everything I believed in. It brought me face to face with not only my Christian beliefs, but with God himself as he walked with me through the darkest valleys and into the light of healing. God personally guided my grief recovery and the lessons

I have learned from him have changed me and my life forever. My confidence in God has been restored through the revelations of who he is and what he has done for me.

I hope by sharing how God carried me through my grief that if you have lost a loved one, particularly a child, you will desire to seek him wholeheartedly in your time of grief, too. If you do, I know you will find him capable of handling your every emotion as you move through your loss. I believe you will discover that God's comfort and personal presence will indeed bring healing to your broken heart.

I also hope that this story might become a tool of encouragement for others who are offering comfort and support to someone who is experiencing deep grief. It is not easy to walk alongside another person who is living with a loss. The journey can seem endless and empathy can run out long before healing comes to the bereaved. Perhaps by looking into my hurting heart and seeing how very lost I was in my own life after my daughter's life was taken, you will more fully understand how paralyzing the pain of loss can be. God can direct you as you grieve with the grieving and provide comfort and hope to those that are so deep in sorrow that they can't see it yet themselves. What a tremendous blessing you will be as you assist them in their grief journey.

Finally, there is a story in the Bible, Luke 10:33-35, called, "The Good Samaritan." It is about a man who comes across another man lying beside the road who has been beaten and robbed. Not only are the two men strangers, but they come from completely different parts of the world. Normally they wouldn't even have taken enough time to greet one another had they passed safely on that same road. But the Samaritan man feels compassion for the stranger who is near death. He places him on his own donkey and carries him to a nearby town where he finds shelter and medical care for the injured man. The Samaritan pays out of his own purse for the man's physical needs before he continues on his journey. Later he returns to check on the injured man and to pay any further expenses towards his care.

I love this story and it comes to mind when I think of helping others who are hurting in grief. For you see, our injuries do not show on the outside, for the most part. Yet the pain we feel in our body, in our heart, in our mind and even in our soul is just as real as the physical injuries of the beaten man lying beside the road. When I first heard that my Angela was gone, in that very moment, it was like receiving a beating on the inside of me. I felt bruised, broken and at points, robbed. My whole world was torn apart. I sincerely felt like I was living in a dying body for a long, long time.

In my story, God was my Good Samaritan, and he faithfully and patiently cared for my needs, not just at the beginning but for the long-run. He brought me back to life, and enabled me to find joy and health once again. I believe with all my heart that he will do the same for anyone who has been beaten up by grief and left by the side of the road to die.

I believe that God intends for each of us to be on the outlook for those needing comfort and care following the loss of a loved one. We can bandage the wounded with loving words and shelter them with a listening heart. God can enable us to help them learn to walk again, and eventually smile and feel hopeful as they begin to move forward in their life. I want to be that kind of "Samaritan" for others. It is my greatest desire that this book will become a little like the Samaritan man for those living with grief and those wanting to come alongside to help them. I hope by sharing about the loss of Angela, who was God's joyous messenger in my life, that the lives of others will be strengthened and encouraged.

CHAPTER 1

Bringing Up Our Blessings

For as long as I can remember, all I ever wanted to be was a mom. On a wintery day in January, a few years after we were married, my dream came true and God blessed my husband, Gordon, and me with our firstborn.

A lot of children are somewhat quiet at their birth, but not our baby. She was screaming before she was fully born and the doctor even commented, saying, "I don't know yet if it is a boy or a girl, but whoever it is...they sure do want to be in charge!" That was our little baby girl, whom we named Angela Joyce. We chose to use Joyce because it was my middle name, my mother's middle name, my mother-in-law's middle name, and even my sister-in-law's middle name. We figured we could just cover everyone if Angela's middle name was Joyce. Joyce means joy, and Angela comes from the word angel, which means God's messenger. So, our Angela Joyce became God's joyous messenger to us.

She was a good baby, a sweet toddler, and a delightful little girl, but we found out early on that she really did like things to be the way she liked them...or else. She learned to talk early, read early, and boss around anyone that she could...early! Raising her we were in for the ride of our lives.

Angela was almost two years old when I became pregnant with what was to be our first boy. She loved sitting beside my enlarged tummy while we read books to the baby. She was eager to share her toys and she was excited to give up the crib for a "big girl bed" in her room. But sleeping in the "big girl bed" wasn't exactly part of her plan. After several nights of putting her to bed only to have her bounce right back out so she could play in her room, over and over again, Gordon and I decided we had to be firm. We tucked her in and kissed her goodnight, but we also promised that staying in her bed to sleep would be far more pleasant than getting up again. It didn't deter her a bit and up she popped. We administered a little pop on her well-padded behind. After several times of following through thusly, we finally heard the precious sound of quiet coming from her bedroom. Upon peeking in, we saw her sound asleep with her head on her bed and her feet planted firmly on the floor. A picture of perfect obedience, almost!

When our baby Joshua was born, Angela was so excited. Daddy brought her to the hospital, where she ran up and down the hall between my room and the baby-viewing window announcing to anyone and everyone, "Come see my new baby bother!" But he wasn't a bother to her at all. She adored him and spent every waking moment chattering to the little guy, getting him toys and offering to rock him. Once I made the mistake of leaving him in his blanket tucked snuggly against the back of the couch while I crossed the room to get something. In a flash, Angela lifted her newborn brother off the couch, turned, and collapsed to the floor under his weight. She didn't lose her grip, and he landed safely in her lap. She sat there smiling, but I was horrified. Her only comment was that he was heavy. I got the playpen out immediately, and from then on she would dance around it, singing constantly while chattering away to Josh, who was lying safely inside it. I am sure one of his earliest recollections includes her smiling face in constant motion above him!

By the time Angela was three years old, we had moved to Bloomington, Indiana where Gordon began working on his Doctorate of Music at Indiana University. One day we were all visiting at his professor's house, and Gordon was playing the piano. Angela, as usual, was dancing around and making up words to sing to the tune Gordon was playing. His professor turned to me and said, "You've got a very musical little girl there and you ought to start her in the music class for young children at the college."

A short time later, the teacher for the Suzuki violin class for children placed the tiniest violin we had ever seen in Angela's little arms. It was love at first sight! She was only three and a half years old, but it was a perfect fit for her. She began weekly lessons that fall, and after only a few months we were told that she needed to participate in a concert in Indianapolis with all the other students. We were skeptical when it was explained to us that Angela would stand on a stage, in the front row with other beginners surrounded by the group of one hundred violin students who were as young as three and as old as eighteen. She was to play "Twinkle, Twinkle, Little Star" along with everyone else, and then, since it was the only tune she knew, she was to sit down on the stage and remain there for the rest of the program. Song after song would go by, and the concert would end with the oldest students playing the most difficult pieces by themselves. We had a hard time imagining our Angela sitting in her spot during the entire concert, so we found seats in the front row in case we would have to grab our rambunctious performer from the stage at a moment's notice. As the program began in the large music hall, Angela stood on stage completely free of fear and proudly played her one-and-only song in perfect unison with the rest of the group. We held our breath as she sat down like a little lady in her shiny black shoes and pretty pink dress, her red hair tied neatly up in pig-tails with matching pink ribbons. She turned away from us so she could see her teacher, and she sat there absolutely motionless and quiet throughout the rest of the performance. We were in total disbelief, but that day we knew one thing for sure: Angela was meant to be a musician.

Another concert took place a year and a half later when Angela was all the more confident in herself as a violinist. This time we relaxed enough to enjoy the music. It really was quite a sight to see one hundred students of all ages playing together in harmony with all the bows going back and forth in perfect unison. Angela was doing just fine and knew many more songs, so she was able to play a lot longer this time. All of a sudden, in the middle of a song the little girl to Angela's left got "off bow." All the bows were in perfect unison except this one child's. Without so much as looking up, Angela reached over with her bow arm and grabbed the little girl's sleeve just long enough so that when the child brought her arm up, she was bowing right along with everyone else. Angela didn't miss a beat with her own bowing. She never even showed as much as a changed expression on her face. She just kept doing what she was supposed to be doing- playing beautifully. She was a mere five years old, and she was a teacher!

As the years went by and our two children grew, so did the size of our family. Angela was seven and Josh was five when we were expecting again. Angela prayed for a little sister, and for months she crossed off each new day on her own calendar, counting the days left until her new sibling was to arrive. One day a few weeks before the appointed time, she came to me with great exasperation and said, "I don't care if it is a boy or a girl, but could you just hurry?" Standing beside her Josh chimed in, "I don't care either Mommy, but couldn't you have a puppy instead?" God saw fit to bless us with another boy, and we named him Bryan. Both Josh and Angela were thrilled with the arrival of their new brother. Josh became the caretaker of Bryan's toys, and Angela moved into the babysitter position early. When I needed to help Josh with something, I would lay baby Bryan at Angela's feet, and she would entertain him perfectly as she practiced her violin for him. He loved it. And later we attributed his love of music in part to her hours of playing for him.

Two years later, our quiver was full with the arrival of Rebecca. This time Angela had left the gender choice up to God but was absolutely delighted with the arrival of her little sister. They were nine years apart by age, but their bond was meant to be strong and sweet. In our little home, the boys shared bunk beds in their bedroom, and a crib was squeezed into Angela's bedroom for baby Rebecca. Right from the beginning Angela made room for the tiny tot who often times dismantled everything in her pre-teen world, but she never seemed to mind. On occasion I would hear their bedroom door open and close, and then I'd hear Rebecca cry as she was placed outside the door when Angela needed alone time. Soon enough their giggles would indicate that all was well and Angela would engage in an activity on Rebecca's level once again.

As they grew and grew and grew, the differences in our children's ages began to test Gordon and me as parents. We were really raising two sets of children. We had the big kids who were just two years apart and who enjoyed similar activities, and the little kids who were also two years apart and who enjoyed all the things that they loved doing together. The stretch of five years between our sets of pals began to bring some challenges. I am sure this isn't unusual for any family to experience, but for us it sometimes brought tension and required some tricky parenting for sure. If we wanted to watch a movie, it had to be entertaining enough for the older kids, but not too scary for the younger ones. Bedtime was two distinct times by the clock, which the younger kids never really appreciated. A road trip brought many opportunities for each child to learn to prefer the other when it came to music choice or places to stop and investigate. But it also came with some complaining and learned tolerance just to keep things civil. Looking back, it was the perfect situation to teach each child to respect the other, to look out for each, and to enjoy being together with a great deal of give and take.

I didn't realize, of course, when the children were all young, what our family would look like a dozen or so years down the road. For example, Rebecca's last year as a preschooler at home was also the year we had one in grade school, one in junior high, and one in high school. When Bryan entered junior high school we had two years of one in grade school, one in junior high school, one in high school, and one in college! That was a real stretch for Gordon and me! Sometimes before heading to my job in the morning the phone would ring. The calls could be a reminder from the grade school to bring cookies for the party at the end of the day, or a frantic call from the junior higher who had forgotten his gym shoes, or a question from the high school student as to whether he could sign up for a special class, or a call from our college gal who was excited about the progress one of her violin students was making. Every day, no matter how we planned ahead, and tried to stay on top of things at home, it seemed that someone needed something done, decided, or dropped off at school. Then there were after school music lessons, scout meetings, and sports activities to attend, plus church youth groups for each person in their own particular age group. We encouraged our children to help earn the things they wanted to have, so we also juggled newspaper routes, babysitting, and their first jobs in town. Taxiing them to-and-fro was nearly a full-time job for Gordon and me as we adjusted our schedules daily according to their needs. Our high school son began his day at zero hour due to his leadership involvement in his business classes and responsibilities there, so our family was up and at it early every weekday. Our college daughter, on the other hand, ended her day of classes, homework, and practicing around midnight. If anyone needed to talk to us just before their day began, or just as it ended, it meant that Gordon and I were on call from dawn to dusk, plus! It was certainly more than we bargained for when they were all youngsters living under one roof. Because Angela's college was as close as it was (an hour and a half as the crow flies), we tried to attend her many concerts, and also get her home for the weekend whenever her schedule allowed. Needless to say, those were the busiest, if not the craziest years of our lives. But looking back, I would not have changed any of it.

No one could have told me how difficult it would be to raise the children that we were so blessed to have, nor could they have conveyed to me how much I would love being a part of each of their busy lives. I wish I could go back and do it again, if only I could change things, and not have worried so much, and spent so much time correcting them. Some of it was necessary, but I would love to have been more prepared for all the crazy times, and not have been such a crazy person in the midst of it all myself! I had not been prepared for the emotional roller coaster these seasons of parenting truly were.

To back up the clock just a bit, one of the hardest things for me as a parent was watching our children experience their own growing pains. For instance, one of the saddest days for our family was when Angela left for college. Angela was eighteen and totally ready for the adventure and the freedom that would accompany it but it was a big change for the rest of us. Everyone had to alter their position in the family somewhat as we adjusted to Angela's absence. To sooth our hearts, and to give her some of the comforts of home while away, we came upon an idea. We assembled a monthly care package for her filling each one with holiday-of-the-month themed gifts and candy. Angela loved getting her love gifts and we loved spending a whole month putting them together. Phone calls took place each Sunday and Angela came home about every month and a half, so little by little, we adjusted. A new normal became our way of life at home, and all was well. The same was true as the time came for each of the other children to grow into their own young adult lives, and leave for the next step beyond home. Before Gordon and I knew what had happened our crowded little home became spacious, somewhat empty, and very, very quiet.

Like all moms, I found that one day can sometimes seem like an eternity, and yet the years still fly by at the speed of light. As the children grew, I had to grow too. God changed my job description from being a hands-on mom to being a mom who parented primarily with her heart, her ears, and occasionally her mouth, when absolutely necessary. It wasn't easy making the adjustment, especially since I had worried about their safety and well-being since the day they were born. But, as it is with most things in life, adjusting to my children being all grown up came without warning, and I really had no choice but to comply as they became more and more independent. My worries were turned into prayers instead, and I actually started to relax.

That is not to say that Gordon and I didn't make mistakes in raising our children. Oh my, we certainly did. We were far from perfect as parents, and if you don't believe me, just ask our children! We made every mistake in the book and created many original ones ourselves. Life's lessons are best recognized in the rearview mirror of time, as it passes by. And, unfortunately, no one gets a "do-over" when it comes to parenting children. I am thankful that God worked in our kids' lives in spite of Gordon and me, and that as the years went by, He saw fit to bless us with amazingly normal, yet extraordinary children.

As our kids graduated from college, and moved into marriage and careers, I too graduated as a mom, and moved forward in my own life. I worked as a Nursery Director at our church for many years overseeing several hundred children in my department and the staff it took to care for them each Sunday. For many years, I had the privilege of helping raise thirteen children from five different families in our home as if we were all just one big happy family, learning, and growing together. I loved each precious child like my own. Eventually though, I stopped doing childcare and took the job of office manager for my husband's life insurance business. Life was different than it had ever been before, but I was fully engaged in it, and enjoying my new found relationships. I even had some time to myself! Still, my greatest joy was always when our kids and their spouses came home, and my family was all together once again for a summer vacation or part of the winter holiday season. One such Christmas, my husband and I laughed as we realized we had children coming home from four different states: one each from

California, Oregon, Idaho and Washington. Two were married and two were in college. We joked that we really needed a jet plane instead of a car to keep up with all of them.

When possible, Gordon and I would leave home to enjoy a three-day weekend drive to Oregon. We loved the chance to attend a concert, sitting with Erik, our son-in-law, while watching his wife, our Angela, play her beloved violin in the Eugene Symphony Orchestra. She was a natural. The next day we would take in a football game at Autzen Stadium where our U of O student and son, Bryan, played in the marching band. We were (and still are) huge Duck fans, and whenever the Ducks lost a football game, we always said, at least the band won! It was a fourteen hour round-trip-by-car kind of a weekend, but we loved every minute of it.

Another such enjoyable weekend trip took us into Idaho where our son, Josh, and his wife lived. They treated us to short road trips around Coeur d'Alene Lake, one of the most beautiful lakes in our country. We fished, picnicked and enjoyed long evenings by their wood stove as we relaxed from our usual duties, and enjoyed their company. One trip in particular took us unexpectedly to the little town where my parents and grandparents were buried. I hadn't visited the cemetery there in several decades. It truly was by God's grace, and Josh's determination, plus prayer for guidance, that we found their grave stones that day. What a blessing it was to be there and take pictures of my son and me together.

Rebecca was our California girl! Because she lived so far away we didn't get to visit her world as much as we desired, but instead we brought her back home to ours whenever possible. We loved our summertime and winter holidays when she flew into town and we got her all to ourselves. Our family was truly blessed when we were able to gather together on campus with Rebecca at her college graduation. She had been in beautiful Southern California for two years. We had all missed her so much, and we loved being able to be there with her that special day. We turned the celebration into a family vacation as we took in Disneyland and the beautiful sunny beaches. Best of all, we spent time with Rebecca and her friends in her tiny dorm room. It was a memory our family will hold onto forever!

Following college graduation Rebecca came back home for the summer for a time of regrouping before starting her Master's program. By the fall, she had settled into a new job and was comfortable being at home with her folks for the time being. Josh and his wife were still living in Idaho and were happily tucked into their routine of work, church involvement, and free time together. Bryan was in his fifth year as a crazy busy music student at the University of Oregon, in Eugene. Angela and her husband, Erik, lived in Vancouver, WA where she was the teacher we always knew she would be, overseeing forty-six violin students in her home studio. Bryan and Angela saw each other the most since she was a member of the symphony in his home town, and she traveled there often for rehearsals and concerts. Our kids were happy, healthy, and doing what they loved most in life...living it to the fullest.

New Year's Eve of 2006 was an amazingly wonderful time spent with everyone coming home for a few days together. We all enjoyed exchanging Christmas gifts, cooking together, and just visiting late into the night, laughing and listening to the sounds of our family. Life was good. All was normal, and if you would have asked me then, I would have said that it was only going to get better and better. Then in an instant, everything changed.

CHAPTER 2
And Then She Was Gone

It was Monday, February 12, 2007, at three-thirty in the morning when I was awakened to loud knocking on our front door. It didn't wake Gordon, so I headed for the door thinking a neighbor must need some kind of help. I spoke through the closed door asking who was there and was surprised to be told it was a policeman. He said my name and asked if he could come in. I told him I would get my husband, and then I would let him in. He agreed. I woke up Gordon, donned my robe, and followed him back to the door, wondering what could possibly bring a police officer to our house. As Gordon opened the door and three officers entered our home, I suddenly knew the reason. Something terrible had happened to one of our children. A sickening calm controlled me as we seated ourselves in our living room on the couch, and I focused on the officer speaking. I will never forget what he said.

"The Oregon State Patrol – 'It is Bryan,' I thought, 'something has happened to Bryan.' – has informed us that Angela Svendsen has been involved in a fatal car accident." My mind raced to keep up with what he was saying. My heart was pounding as I held my breath, while the officer's words sank in. The word "fatal" hung in the air as I grappled with my thoughts and his words. Angela, it was my Angela; she was dead? My Angela was gone? No, how could that be? I couldn't comprehend it. I was her mom. I would have known if such a horrible thing had happened to her. She had just celebrated her thirty-first birthday exactly two weeks ago, and I had talked with her on the phone only last Thursday. How could this be real?

The next few minutes and hours were a blur. While Gordon spoke with the officers I hurried downstairs, and woke our youngest telling her the terrible news which still seemed so unreal to me. I walked around in a fog, crying. Gordon and I were trying to think and make plans to get to our son-in-law's house, five hours away, as soon as possible. We called Josh and his wife and told them what had happened. We explained we would be driving to Angela's house right away. We told Josh that we would make plans to fly him and his wife there to join us in a day or two. Then we called Bryan, whom we were very concerned about since he lived alone and was so far from any other family member. He called his pastor, and to-gether they met with friends at their church for support. We packed hurriedly and began the five-hour trip to Vancouver. God provided a heavy gray fog for us to drive through that morning. Normally, I would have found this to be very unnerving, but that day it felt like God wrapped us in his billowing robe and was holding us close as we headed to Angela's home. God was most certainly with us as we started out on our journey of grief.

As the day wore on, we learned more about the details of the collision. Angela had been in a car Sunday night, February 11th, with two other women, all members of the Eugene Symphony Orchestra. They were returning to Vancouver from a symphony rehearsal in Eugene late in the evening. Kjersten Oquist, the symphony's prin-cipal violist, was driving. Angela, the symphony's principal second violinist, was seated in the front passenger seat next to her. And Kelly Gronli, the symphony's principal oboist, was seated behind Angela. They were headed north on I-5 near Albany, Oregon. Another young woman, who was attempting to head north and who was driving under the influence of alcohol, mistakenly took a southbound exit, the wrong way onto the Northbound freeway. She was in the same lane and headed straight towards the car carrying the three women. She was driving too fast for either vehicle to maneuver away from the other. Angela and Kjersten were killed instantly in the collision. Miraculously, Angela's seat pushed back protecting Kelly and sparing her life. The drunk driver in the oncoming car also survived the crash.

The next few days were filled with meetings with the funeral director, making plans for two separate memorial services, and spending time with our son-in-law, Erik, his family, and our other children. Everyone was doing everything they could to make the best of the worst thing any of us could ever imagine happening. Because the women involved in the collision were members of the Eugene Symphony, and because the collision was caused by a wrong-way drunk driver, the event was widely broadcasted by the media. Angela's husband, Erik, was interviewed several times in their living room by television and newspaper people. Proceedings against the drunk driver were initiated by the state of Oregon immediately. We were told that a criminal trial would be set for some time in the future. We began to realize that this nightmare would be a very, very long one.

Five days after our daughter's death, we celebrated her life with a memorial service in our hometown. Each member of our family took their turn to speak about their relationship with Angela. They shared about her humor, her love of teaching and of music, her faith in God, and her zest for life and all it held for her. There were smiles, laughter, and tears, and that day, through it all, God began the process of healing our hearts. Nine days later a similar memorial service took place in Angela's hometown. Nearly all of her forty-six students, ages three to forty plus, took the stage together and played "Twinkle, Twinkle, Little Star" to honor their beloved teacher. This was not only the first song she learned so long ago on her own violin, but it was also the first song she taught each of her precious students in her own studio where she had taught for over nine years. Both memorial services were filled to capacity, and both became places where God began to work through the tragedy of losing our Angela to bring hope and healing to everyone.

As a mom, I have experienced every kind of feeling that comes with losing a child. I have lived through days I thought I couldn't live through. I have sat through a criminal trial that found a young single mother guilty of recklessly taking the life of two other women and injuring a third. I have found it in my heart to forgive this woman and to pray for her to find a relationship with God. Yet, I have wept tears of relief at the sentencing when justice was served on behalf of Angela, Kjersten and Kelly with the conviction of a long prison term against the drunk driver.

I have crawled into God's lap millions of times for comfort, and at the same time wrestled with Him as to why this had to happen in the first place. He has not failed to comfort me, to understand me, and to help me endure the pain of a mother's hurting heart. God has shown me he will be with me always, even during sleepless nights and agonizingly long days. God has used every opportunity to teach me so many things about life here on this earth, and about what I am supposed to be doing while I live out mine. And God has helped me process the loss of Angela in so many different and very personal ways.

One of the most difficult things to get past in my early grief was the picture in my mind of the car crash itself. I was not there at the scene, of course, but the newspapers had printed pictures of both cars following the incident. The reality of the oncoming car crashing into the car my daughter was in was very evident in those photographs. Further description came out in the criminal trial against the drunk driver who had caused the tragic event. That information, plus the newspaper photos and my vivid imagination, seared the scene into my brain and my mother-heart.

We had been told by authorities who were at the scene that Angela had died instantly in the crash. I knew and believed, as did the rest of my family, that she had slipped from that car into heaven in a moment of time. We were grateful she had not suffered pain physically or any other way. Her death was too sudden for that. We knew heaven had become her home instantly, and that was the one blessing we clung to in our loss of her. But even so, for months following her death, throughout the day, and especially at night when I tried to sleep, the image of her seeing the headlights of the oncoming car, and then lying dead in the front seat, filled my mind and brought immediate tears and a feeling of brokenness. I just couldn't get past it. I would be fine one moment, and then the next I would see her there, and the pain would hit me along with the tears. Everyone said grief would ease with time, but no one had explained to me how to empty my mind of those horrifying images.

One day, while sitting alone, I was again thinking about the crash. The thought came to me that if God had frozen time a few seconds before that car touched Angela, and if he had then turned to me and said, "You or her?" my immediate response would have been, "Me, please dear God, get her out of there, and take me!" I wouldn't have had to give it a second thought. I loved her so much I would have gladly taken her place. At that very moment, as I sat in my living room just thinking, it was as if God said to me, "That is what I did. I took her place...on the cross." Wow, that thought stretched my brain and took me immediately to Calvary where I saw Jesus on the cross with new realization and tremendous appreciation for the sacrifice he made there. I had known for years that Jesus died for my sins to make a way for me to live eternally in heaven instead of facing eternal death. I knew that, and believed that, with all my heart. And if you had asked me if I believed that Jesus died for my kids too, I would have answered, of course he did. But that day, sitting there alone with my thoughts, the cross and the car crash came together for me. As much as I loved Angela, I could not have intervened and rescued her from death in that car. But Jesus had made the choice two thousand years before to make a way to rescue her from eternal death. For the first time I realized that it was not just obedience to God his Father that placed Jesus Christ on the cross, but it was absolute and desperate love for every single person in the human race that enabled him to hang there and die there. I wept as I understood the depth of the love Jesus had for my precious daughter, so much so, that he would choose to die for her. Tears of gratitude flowed with the understanding that the immense love I had for her was surpassed by Jesus' love for her.

That revelation filled my mind, my heart and my soul. I was overwhelmed. At that very moment, and from that point on, the image of the car crash became connected to the knowledge of her escape from it. The terror it always brought to my heart turned into an all-encompassing gratitude for the very personal love I knew God had for Angela. The cross, a part of God's redemptive plan, became a place of new appreciation for me and a place of worship. In my mind, when I see the cross, I now see that crumpled car at the foot of it, and I know, just as Jesus is no longer on that cross, neither is Angela trapped by death in that car. Because of his sacrifice and her faith in him, both are free from physical death and, better yet, eternal death, and both are safe in heaven for ever.

If ever I could have denied the existence of my heavenly Father before losing Angela, I cannot do so now. For I have seen him, heard him, and felt him move in my life. I know for a fact that he cradled Angela as he carried her broken body from that twisted wreckage and introduced her to the glories of heaven. I know heaven is real; I understand that life is precious and short, and I must live it as God reveals it to me. But I also know that compared to an eternity in heaven, my life is but a vapor. I know there is a purpose in every-thing, and that no matter how chaotic life may be, no matter what happens, God is in control, and he will bring victory and peace to anyone who looks to him for it.

If someone were to ask me how many children I have or some-thing about my kids, I would respond proudly that I am a mother of four. I would tell them about three of my children, where they live and something about what they are doing presently. And then I would tell them that my oldest child resides in heaven. I would comment that there is no doubt in my mind that she is teaching violin to any person there that wants to learn it, and probably to a few who aren't too sure about it. I would have to say that when I see a rainbow I think of a poem she wrote about rainbows for me when she was a child. I would tell them that when my heart hurts so much I can't stand it, I imagine one of her hugs, and I think about her smile. I would proudly say that I am blessed to be a mother, and that God is capable of holding a mother's broken heart in his gentle and loving hands. I know, because he is holding mine.

CHAPTER 3
My Own Miracle

Six months following Angela's death, sleeping was still a struggle. Most of the time I could fall asleep quickly but then would awake partway through the night, and just lie there exhausted but unable to fall asleep again. Whether it was the exhaustion, or the quiet darkness, it was in these moments that I felt the ache of loss and dread of living without my daughter to be the strongest. And it was in these moments that turned into hours, that I felt the furthest from God, that the unanswerable "why" of the whole miserable situation stuck in my head, and that my faith felt tested. To give into this kind of thinking was to relive the horribleness of the event over and over again. To head backwards into the deepest part of grief brought uncontrollable crying that left me physically hurting. This cycle had to be broken or I knew I would break.

Because of this, I had begun a routine of pulling myself from bed, making a cup of warm cocoa, and settling down in a chair in the living room with my Bible. My brain was my baby, and I was determined to read it to sleep, and then return to bed without waking it, so I could hopefully sleep until morning. But one particular night, though my brain was wide awake, my body just didn't want to budge. I decided to focus on the Bible without getting out of bed and see if that would work. A question popped into my head, and I

wondered what people in the Bible had done when they had faced
the most horrific thing in their lives.

Daniel immediately came to mind as I had recently read his
story to the children at my church. He was an Israelite who lived in
exile in Babylon, under the authority of King Darius, a Mede, who
was anything but a godly king. King Darius appointed Daniel as
one of three administrators to help govern the kingdom. Daniel's
amazing leadership skills and personality allowed him to rise above
the others in the eyes of the king. Therefore, out of jealousy, the
other administrators and leaders created a devious plan to get rid of
Daniel. They went as a group to King Darius and convinced him
that he was worthy of being worshipped by everyone in the kingdom. They suggested that he issue an edict stating that if anyone
prayed to any other god or man except the king, that person should
be thrown into the lions' den and be devoured! King Darius was so
flattered by their allegiance that he agreed to their plan and decreed
it as law.

In the meantime, even as a foreigner in Babylon, Daniel had
continued to be a faithful follower of his God, the God of Israel.
As was his custom, he prayed three times a day as he knelt beside
his open window facing Jerusalem. His adversaries were counting
on the fact that he would continue to do so...and they were not
disappointed. When the bad guys went to King Darius and tattled
on Daniel, the king was saddened because he really liked Daniel.
He tried his best to wiggle out of his own decree without success.
Eventually he found himself standing with Daniel near the den of
the hungry lions. King Darius told Daniel that he hoped his God
would rescue him. With that Daniel was tossed into the den. The
Bible says the king went home and didn't eat or sleep.

Now I can picture Daniel as he was thrown into that deep,
dark lions' den. I could imagine his heart beating wildly as he
landed hard, and stood surrounded by real-live lions. I had never
thought about how horrible it would be to be eaten alive. I would

have fainted, but the Bible says nothing of what Daniel did or how he felt. It only says that the next day, when asked by the king if he was alive, he responded by saying, "My God sent his angel and he shut the mouths of the lions. They have not hurt me, because I was found innocent in his sight." Daniel 6:22. Daniel was most certainly a man of prayer, so I can assume he prayed that night. If it had been me, and I had not fainted I would have prayed too, constantly, that whole night long.

Still wide awake, my mind jumped to Jonah. His story gives me the shudders, as I happen to have a personal fear about drowning. I am a pretty good swimmer, so the thought of being overtaken by water enough to drown makes me uncomfortable. Jonah was asked by God to go to the wicked city of Ninevah to preach a message of repentance to the people who lived there. He did not want to go. Instead he chose to try and run away from God. He headed in the opposite direction and boarded a ship that would take him even further away from God's mission for him. Surprisingly enough, God saw what Jonah was up to and he sent a huge storm that threatened the lives of everyone on the ship. Jonah fesses up to his rebellion against God when the shipmates question him. He tells them to throw him overboard and the storm will cease. They do, and it does.

I really can't imagine how Jonah felt as he was tossed off the boat into the stormy sea. Again, I would have fainted, and drowned unknowingly. But not Jonah, he tries to keep his head above water, as the raging sea around him begins to calm. Then things get even worse. A large fish comes right at him, and he feels its jaws close around him. I think I would rather drown than be swallowed alive. Since Jonah wasn't in good terms with God at the time, maybe he didn't pray, maybe he expected death to come. He certainly didn't expect to be spat out onto dry ground, and to walk away to tell about it. But that's exactly what happened. The experience changes Jonah's heart and mind and he fulfills God's mission with great passion which ends up saving all of Ninevah from destruction.

Finally, I thought about the Bible story that I imagined to be one of the very worst: that of the three Israelites facing the fiery furnace. The Bible says that the men who were with them died from the heat of the furnace as they walked the three bound men towards it. I can't imagine that these guys expected to live, but the Bible also says that just before they were tossed into the inferno they told the king that they believed God would save them from him, and rescue them from the fire. And God did just that. The Bible says that after the three men were tossed down into the furnace, the king peered into it astonished! "Then King Nebuchadnezzar leaped to his feet in amazement, and asked his advisers 'Weren't there three men that we tied up and threw into the fire?' They replied, 'Certainly, O king.' He said, 'Look! I see four men walking around in the fire, unbound and unharmed, and the fourth looks like a son of the gods.' Nebuchadnezzar then approached the opening of the blazing furnace and shouted, 'Shadrack, Meshack and Abednego, servants of the Most High God, come out! Come here!'" Daniel 3:24–26. When the three men came out of the furnace everyone saw that the fire had not harmed them. Their hair was not singed and their clothing wasn't even scorched. They didn't even smell like they had been anywhere near a fire! You see, prior to being thrown into the furnace Shadrack, Meshack and Abednego had been disobeying King Nebuchadnezzar. The king had demanded that everyone in his kingdom worship his golden idols, and serve his gods. They were in a similar situation as Daniel had been in. They refused, and so they had to face the king's wrath and fiery punishment. What a test of faith, and what a witness to the faithfulness of God. It completely changes the king's heart. He becomes a believer in God, and demands that all the golden idols be destroyed across the kingdom. He further decrees that anyone who says anything against the God of Shadrack, Meshack and Abednego will also be destroyed. What a story.

As I pondered these three separate events, and the men involved in them, I realized that in each case they were experiencing the very worst thing that had ever happened to them thus far in their lives. I could sort of relate to that, even though my life hadn't been the one in danger. Also, in each story I realized that God rescued the men with a miracle designed specifically for them, and their situation. In fact, the whole point of each story is not just the personal faith in God that is revealed in each person's life, but the miracles God brought about for them. Those miracles proved to them personally, and to everyone who would ever read about them, that God was real, and that when any situation seemed to be out of control– God was in control and that he cares enough to rescue his own. If any person were to ask about why these situations had to happen the answer would have to be, because without the scariest moments of their lives, none of these men would have experienced the miracle of God's rescue, and his personal love for them.

That's where I was, experiencing the worst thing I had ever imagined happening in my life. Now, the question before me was, could I trust God for the miracle he had in store for me? Could I trust him to rescue me from grief, and sorrow, and the pain of losing Angela? Could I let God use every part of what had happened to her to be a way of showing himself more personally to me, and to others through me? I hadn't thought of this before.

As I lay there, truly wide awake, I felt God's arms around me. I cried, but it was a different cry, one that was letting go of pain instead of feeling its grasp. God was there rescuing me from the horror of it all. My miracle was taking place not in a pit, not in the depths of the sea, not in a fiery inferno, but deep within my heart. In the future when sleep would not come I could still rest in God's protection, and love for me. Just as he helped those men overcome fear for themselves, turn it into faith, and trust in him, God could do the same for me. Then slowly, over time, his miracle of rescue would bring the healing I desperately needed.

CHAPTER 4
Heavenly Homes

One evening I was sitting in my living room, looking out my deck door into the darkness, and I observed tiny lights coming from homes across town. Even though the distance from me to them was many miles crossing the valley, the river, and up the hills, I could see them clearly. As I sat watching the flickering lights dancing on the hillside, I thought about all the people who lived in the houses. I had friends who lived in those houses, and though I couldn't see them, or hear them, or readily talk to them from my living room without the aid of a phone, still, I knew they were there, snug in their homes, for the lights I saw were proof of that.

Then the thought came to me– what if the stars in the sky are just like those lights dancing on the hillside? What if God placed the stars there to twinkle and glow as if they were lights from millions of heavenly homes?

I think about heaven often since Angela has been there over a year now. She has joined my parents, my grandparents, and other relatives and friends of mine who reside on the other side of eternity. I miss them all so very much, especially my daughter. The thought of being able to see the lights from her heavenly home instantly warmed my heart, and made her seem less far away.

Of course, the stars are not really the twinkling lights from heavenly homes, but from now on I will think of them as such. And who knows, maybe in the grand scheme of things, that is why God sprinkled the stars across the night sky in the first place. Maybe he is letting us know that heaven is just across the way, and those already there are safely tucked into their heavenly homes with him. What a blessing to think about heaven in a new light, and to consider it as if it weren't so very far away. God is so good, that even in the darkness of life I can say, "Thanks for leaving the lights on!"

Revelation 22:16 "I AM...the bright Morning Star."

John 14:2 & 3 "In my Father's house, are many rooms: if it were not so, I would have told you. I am going there to prepare a place for you. And if I go and prepare a place for you, I will come back and take you to be with me that you also may be where I am."

II Corinthians 5:1 "Now we know that if the earthly tent we live in is destroyed, we have a building from God, an eternal house in heaven, not built by human hands."

CHAPTER 5
Layered Grief

A few weeks following Angela's death, I attempted to get back into life as usual, as did the rest of my family. Our grown children had returned to their homes, their jobs, and their lives, never to be the same, but needing to do the same things that they had done in life prior to losing their sister. My husband returned to work much sooner than I did, as he didn't have the luxury of taking his time, and he said that getting back into a routine was helpful in the overall need of just plain getting back to normal. We would all find, further down the road, that it did indeed take time before any of us could say that life was normal again, or that we were normal within it. Grief, as we had been told early on, is hard work and it does take time, lots and lots of time to make the journey through it.

As I attempted to return to my normal routine of housekeeping, cooking meals, doing laundry, paying bills, grocery shopping, and numerous other chores that usually were accomplished without much thought or concern, I found that I just didn't have the emotional energy or physical stamina to do very much without falling into a heap in the nearest chair. Tears still came easily, but more than anything, the wrenching ache in my stomach, and golf-ball sized lump in my throat prevented me from focusing successfully on whatever chore I was trying to get done. I knew it was grief that was overwhelming me, and my life, and I knew, as stated earlier, that grief was hard work, and that grief really does hurt, physically, mentally, emotionally, and spiritually. I just wasn't sure exactly what I was supposed to do to move through the process in a healthy way. I longed to be without the pain of loss that I felt constantly, but I had no idea how to rid myself of it.

I tried leaving the radio on all day long, set to the Christian station. I found the sermons I was listening to were helpful, and amazingly specific to the need of my heart, but the songs brought buckets of tears, and seemed to echo the loss of my daughter in each refrain, no matter the song choice. Wanting to talk with her, to hear her voice, and to know that she was just going about her daily business as usual permeated my thoughts and was reflected in most everything I heard and saw during the early days and weeks of grieving. Some days I did better if I just chose to spend the day in quiet thought, without the intrusion of music, or the voices of others who, though they didn't know it, seemed to be trying to pull me back into life as it should be. But then again, my brain was on auto redial and seemed bent on replaying the trauma that had happened. So the peace and quiet outside my brain couldn't compete with the noise inside of it.

I had been given books on grief or about others who had experienced a tragedy in their lives, and I really did try to sit down and read some of them. But the words seemed so heavy, and it was nearly impossible to have any empathy with anyone else's loss but my own. Looking back on those first few months without Angela, I became the most selfish person I had ever been in my life. I wrapped my grief around me like a heavy quilt, and I didn't let anyone or anything come between it and me. Though it was cumbersome at best, it became my comfort, and my companion, and unfortunately it kept me from moving very far away from the initial shock and sting of losing my daughter. I had no clue that I was actually wrapping her broken, lifeless body in my grief quilt, holding her as close to me as possible. I just didn't want to let go, for fear that I would be letting go of her.

Before long I needed to return to my job as Nursery Director at my church. Everyone where I worked had been more than understanding in my absence. I was able to work at my desk using the computer, but using the phone to contact volunteers for nursery help on the upcoming Sunday was very difficult. I felt like my voice wavered even when I was in complete control of it. And though I was not in tears, I was certain that it sounded that way, and that I was making everyone I spoke to very uncomfortable. All I wanted to do was shut the door to my office and sit at my desk undisturbed. Staff meetings were also difficult, as the lump in my throat and pain in my stomach got worse when I was in the company of others. Curiously enough, even though I couldn't pray out loud or speak about any topic at hand without losing it, the ache of my heart came pouring out of my mouth constantly. I felt compelled to share whatever I was experiencing in my grief at that time. The amazing people on our church staff were so patient. They listened without much choice, I imagine, to whatever gushed forth from within me. Whether it was something I felt God was showing me, or just more information I was learning about the incident itself, or the trial against the drunk driver that took more than a year and a half to come to completion, they listened. Looking back, I don't know how my coworkers stretched their empathy as long as they did. They are to be commended for their compassion and their ability to grieve with the grieving, as the Bible suggests. They really were a huge part of my grief recovery whether they ever knew it or not.

One day, quite a few months after being back at work, our staff finished a meeting, and we were all milling back to our own offices. I was beginning to think that the grief I felt was a life sentence, and I said something about it to one of the women I worked with. I told her it seemed to me that nothing was changing to make it any better, and that I actually was feeling worse than I had in prior months. I told her I thought everyone in my family was doing so much better than I was, and I didn't know why. She stopped in her tracks, and said to me, "Kathy, you are experiencing layers of grief, and that makes the loss of your daughter so much harder." I am not sure now that those were her exact words, but it was her meaning, and I remember they hit me like a ton of bricks. The concept had never crossed my mind. I must have stood there expressing that thought because she continued on telling me that she knew it wasn't the first time I had lost someone I loved. She said that I would need to see the grief of all my losses wrapped together, and begin to heal from the inside out of each loss. With that she was at her office door, and we parted ways. I went to my office, shut the door, and sat down trying to comprehend the message I had just received.

I had never heard of layered grief. Nor had anyone else ever mentioned that those grieving from multiple losses may indeed have leftover grief from one loss to another that would complicate and lengthen the healing time of the last grief experienced. It made sense, and it was something I needed to think and pray about. I didn't realize it at the time, but my caring friend gave me a key to my getting on a healthy path for my grief journey. I needed a starting place, and that day I found one.

Back home, I took out the pile of books about grief that our family had collected rather quickly after word spread about Angela's death. Everything from small pamphlets tucked into sympathy cards to entire books written about the stages of grief had found their way to our home. We had books about heaven, about those who had experienced loss of one kind or another, and specifically about other parents who had lost a child, just as we had. Those who had given us the books were people who had either dealt with what we were going through or at the very least could understand the depth of loss we were experiencing. The love, hope, and encouragement that came with each gift was indeed a blessing, but until my friend's comment about my layered grief, as mentioned earlier, I had primarily ignored the pile of books at home. But now they seemed like a good place to start to gain insight into my own grief journey.

Little by little, as I read about grief and how people grieve differently, I began to learn that I had never really fully grieved over the death of the loved ones in my past, at least not to the degree that I was experiencing with the death of Angela. I also learned that when you avoid grief or just try to move on with your life in spite of it, that grief gets tucked deep down into your soul, and you are really only delaying the explosion or implosion that is sure to come from it one day. I needed to go backwards before I could go forwards. I needed to rethink the losses I had experienced, and let grief move through me before I could move through it. Thus began the hard work of grieving that I had been hearing about. And thus began my journey backwards to a time long ago in my life.

CHAPTER 6
My Grandfather

My father's father, my Grandpa Esmay, lived with my grandmother above a small grocery store they owned in St. Maries, Idaho. As very young children, my siblings and I loved to go with our parents to visit them. We were allowed to "play store" amongst the small town shoppers who came to buy their goods at this mom and pop market. We would fill our carts with packages of paper products, canned goods or boxed items (things we couldn't hurt, Grandma had said) and shop all over the little store. We pushed things around on the shelves making little places we could crawl into for our homes, and we pretended to live there. As long as we put everything back in its place, we could do whatever we wanted. The shoppers didn't seem to mind passing shelves with arms and legs sticking out of them, and they always received a cheery hello from us as they went by. I have fond memories of lying in one of those little crawl spaces, and listening to the conversations coming from the people sitting in the chairs around the big wooden barrel of peanuts near the sales counter. The unshelled peanuts were offered to all customers whether they came in for groceries or just a chat with the grocer himself. They were free of charge as were the conversations and the laughter that filled the little store, indicating that just being there was well worth the trip. I had a little apron with my name on it, and from time to time Grandma would ask me to come put it on so I could sell candy from the shelf behind the old cash register. I stood up on a small box, and took each person's order as they willingly handed over their pennies for a handful of the sweet stuff. I loved that old cash register and had to push with all my might to make the handle of it go down to ring a sale. I felt so grown up doing so. From my spot behind the counter I could also see Grandpa lift out the large rolls of bologna as he sliced off just the exact number of slices each customer wanted. It all seemed so magical at the time.

Grandpa was also an artist, and usually had an extremely large oil painting, partially finished, leaning against a window in the front of the store. As he had time, he would work on the painting, sometimes taking a year or so to finish it. Charlie Russell's collection of Native American chiefs and their horses was Grandpa's inspiration, and he copied many of them for his own enjoyment. His only challenge was the trouble he had drawing the right perspective of the horse's legs in his paintings. When our family would come to visit, it wasn't unusual for us to see an amazing painting with dozens of chiefs wearing colorful headdresses sitting upon their beautiful steads, except for the fact that the horses had no legs. Grandpa left that part to my mother, also an artist, who would happily stand for hours at his easel and fill in each missing leg perfectly. It was really something to watch the two of them as they completed the picture together.

When I was in grade school Grandma and Grandpa Esmay came to our home one particular Christmas. Grandpa gave me my first large picture Bible, and told me the most important story in it was the story of Creation. I don't know why he thought that, but it has always been one of my favorites too, probably because of him. He was the first person other than my parents to make a spiritual impact on my life. I will always be grateful for that memory of him. As it turned out, Grandpa Esmay was also the first person I had known, and loved so very much, that brought me to the initial experience of losing a loved one.

It was the summer of 1969, and I was sixteen years old. One

of my best friends and I convinced our parents to let us take a bus
from our hometown in Washington, and travel to California where
both she and I had relatives living in the same community. We felt
we were ready for an adventure such as this, and our families in
California were excited for us to visit them. Amazingly enough,
our parents agreed to our traveling vacation, and after earning our
bus fare and planning out the details of our trip, we headed south.
I was to stay with my Aunt Marion and my Uncle Carle who were
my dad's brother and sister-in-law, and my friend was staying with
her aunt and uncle. We would meet a few times for some fun on
the beach together, and then after our two week vacation was over,
my aunt and uncle planned to drive us all back home and enjoy a
summertime visit with my family.

My friend and I arrived safe and sound at our California destina-
tion and were enjoying our grownup experience to the fullest when
sad news arrived at the home of my uncle. My grandfather had died
suddenly. Our trip ended abruptly as we all drove quickly back to
Washington to be with my family. My grandfather's funeral is still
a blur to me, but watching the pain and grief my dad and my uncle
experienced hit me hard. I had never lost a loved one before, nor had
I ever watched someone else grieve for someone they cared so much
about. My own grief was hidden in the grief of my parents, and for
whatever reason I don't recall ever talking about it with anyone. Life
just went on without my Grandpa Esmay being a part of it.

Grandpa had left a second will written on a piece of paper tucked
into a drawer that Grandma found a few days following his death.
Evidently, whatever he wrote complicated the process of settling his
will, and since my dad was assigned to be executor of the estate,
he spent many hours helping my grandmother sort everything out
legally. We lived about three hours from Grandma, so Dad helped
her over the phone as much as possible. This all took place in June
of 1969, and as I recall, the year ended with the estate still in limbo,
at least it seems that way to me now.

CHAPTER 7
My Dad

The year also ended with Dad beginning to have some really terrible headaches. We used to take home movies at birthdays and other holidays, and I still have the ones we took that Christmas back in 1969. They show our father sitting on the couch watching his children open their presents while he is rubbing the back of his neck constantly. The headaches continued to worsen, and get closer together. Then one evening, on January 13, 1970, Dad collapsed in our home.

My brother, Ron, came hurriedly to my bedroom where I was doing my homework. He told me he had heard Dad groan and fall in our bathroom, and that the door was locked. Our mother was bowling with her bowling team at another town about a half-hour from our hometown. So Ron came to me, the oldest person aside from Dad. I ran to our bathroom, and indeed the door was locked. I found a small key we had made from a nail hanging on the wall that opened the door. My little sisters were famous for locking that door behind them when they left the bathroom, leaving no one inside, so we had rigged up the "key" to open it. I fumbled with the nail and finally the door unlocked. Inside I found my father lying on his back in convulsions. My mom and I were Girl Scouts, and we had just recently taken a class in first aid and CPR. Everything I had learned flooded my mind, and at the same time seemed overwhelmingly confusing. I grabbed a toothbrush, and placed the handle in Dad's mouth remembering that I needed to keep his tongue down flat, and I told Ron to call for an ambulance.

Soon the volunteers in our small town arrived with the ambulance. Dad had stopped his convulsions and was trying to grasp the situation at hand. I was asked to call our mom and find out where she wanted the ambulance to go. The choice was a very small clinic in the town where she already was, a half hour away, or our family doctor and the hospital that was about an hour away. She said she would meet the ambulance at the hospital. The volunteers placed my father on a gurney and placed him into the ambulance. I asked our pastor, who was one of the volunteers present, if he would call his wife to come be with my siblings so I could ride with my dad. I told my sisters and brothers everything would be okay. I grabbed some papers Mom had asked me to bring to her, and I scrambled into the front of the ambulance. As it pulled away from my house, I had no idea that very shortly everything my family knew to be normal in life would change.

My father underwent some testing at the hospital that night, and without further convulsing, was able to return home with Mom a few days later. I will never forget the hugs he gave me and my brothers and sisters when he walked back into our house. He told us how very proud he was of each of us, but all I could think was how thankful I was that he was okay. I was glad the trauma had passed, and life in our little family in our little town could go back to being uneventful.

Washtucna was a very small, but thriving, community of about 350 people. We moved there the summer of 1959 just before I was to begin first grade. My youngest sibling was born that summer completing our family of seven, and thus beginning our life in the town we would always remember as home sweet home.

My dad was the grade school principal and the sixth grade classroom teacher at the same time. Our school was one long building with the grade school classrooms at one end, junior high in the middle near the gym, the cafeteria and library next to the gym, and the high school classrooms at the other end of the building. My mom taught high school art classes, and helped teach kindergarten. She was also the city clerk for the mayor of Washtucna. Mom and Dad were both active in our community church where Mom taught a preschool Sunday school class, and Dad led the adult Sunday school class. Dad was a Boy Scout leader for the older boys, and Mom led a Girl Scout troop for grade school girls. Both took turns serving on the PTA board as needed. Participating in every way in our community, and supporting the activities of their children, were high on our parents' priority list. The fourteen years that our family nestled in Washtucna were like the "Leave It to Beaver" years, when all the parents came to the school for the Friday night football or basketball games, depending on the time of year, and every high school student turned out for sports or band or both. You saw your friends at school all day, at church on Sunday, and at every community event that took place. My parents were just regular folks raising a large but regular family, just like everyone else.

We lived on the edge of town, and our property had a barn, a small pasture, and a huge yard around our house. We always had a cow that provided fresh milk and calved annually, and once that calf grew up it ended up in our freezer as packaged meat for the upcoming year. We also raised rabbits and chickens, had multiple litters of cats and kittens, and had our family dog, Puddles. We had a big garden, huge trees that provided lots of leaf raking in the fall, and if we ran out of things to do at home, the hills surrounding our hometown were just on the other side of our pasture fence. In the wintertime when the hills were covered in snow, sledding trails were in constant use, and the bonfire at the bottom of the hill became a gathering place for kids and adults alike. In the summertime we exchanged long pieces of cardboard for the sleds, and the adventures continued. As childhoods go, ours was filled with fun, responsibility, and hours of working together as a family on one project or another.

The only challenge I ever found to living where we lived were the rattlesnakes we encountered every summer in our yard. I prayed many long hours for protection from them, as I was scared to death of the danger they presented to my family. Many were the times one of us children came screaming into the house to our mother with the news that we had found one. Dad worked at a grain elevator each summer earning much-needed extra income for the family so Mom was left to be the snake-killer, and she did her job well. She was our heroine as she used a shovel, hoe, or rock to end the life of the slithering creatures, one by one, as they dared to leave the hillside, and slink onto our property. I could never have done what she did, but it certainly added to the admiration I had for her, and for my dad, as they did whatever it took to make life safe and good for our family.

Dad taught each of his own children in his sixth grade classroom except my youngest sister, Jenny. Since I was the oldest child, I was the first to have this honor. Instead of calling him "Dad" at school, we had to refer to him as "Mr. Esmay." It didn't seem odd to us, and he thoroughly enjoyed teaching us for a year as we became old enough to be in his classroom. Karen was a student in his class the year he collapsed at home, and I am sure it was very difficult for her to watch him at home, as well as at school, as he grew more and more ill.

Finally, after weeks of continued medical testing, a diagnosis was given. Dad had a brain tumor. That information did not mean the same to us back then as it means to people today. Cancer was certainly recognized, and understood as something very scary, but our family had no personal experience with it. It was explained to us that Dad would undergo surgery to remove the tumor and would have to take some time off from school to recover. Then we would see what would happen. It all sounded like we had plenty of time to figure it out. But time was exactly what we didn't have. Three weeks after Dad collapsed he was scheduled for surgery. That morning before school, each of us kids hugged him and said goodbye assuring him we would be good for Grandma and Grandpa Rumelhart who had come to stay with us. I will never forget how weak and ill my father looked as I hugged him and told him goodbye. My brother and I were playing basketball later that week, and so my Dad's final words to me were, "Good luck!" And with that I headed off to school, and he and Mom headed to the hospital in Spokane.

That was a Monday, and the day was long as I waited for news at school that all had gone as planned. The high school principal finally came to my classroom to tell me that the surgery had gone well, and Dad was doing great. I was so relieved. But as the week continued he seemed to get worse, not better. Finally, on Thursday evening Mom called us at home saying Dad wasn't doing well, that he was experiencing some paralysis on one side. I spoke to her on the phone, and she was crying. I had never heard or seen my mother cry except at my grandfather's funeral. I could hardly sleep that night.

I remember kneeling down beside my bed to say my prayers. As I prayed for my father's recovery a tremendous uneasiness came over me. I had been praying for Dad's healing for weeks and had been thanking God that soon he would be well and back to normal. The uneasiness I felt that night grew worse, and for the first time I had the thought that my Dad might die. It was like cold water in my face, for I really hadn't considered that before. I had been a Christian for only a few years, but God was so very real to me, and I knew and believed that He was in complete control. I knew my father trusted God completely with everything including his own life. Mom had told me on the phone that Dad had prayed the Lord's Prayer with her just before his surgery. So that night I prayed that God's will would be done in Dad's life, knowing that it could go either way, and I left it at that and crawled into bed.

The next morning was Friday the thirteenth, the day before Valentine's Day, and I was supposed to go on a bus trip to a basketball tournament after school with my brothers. They played on the boys A-team and I played on the girls B-team. I was looking forward to the tournament, and to the Valentine's Day parties at school that we would have before leaving on the bus later that day. I was coming out of the bathroom after getting ready for school when Mom walked into the house completely unexpectedly. My grandmother, her mom, was standing in the kitchen. We were all gathering there getting ready for breakfast. Mom stood still in the middle of the room and my grandmother gasped, saying, "No, Joanne!" My Mom motioned to me to be calm in front of my younger siblings, and then she told us that our father had died that morning. I was paralyzed with shock, as were we all.

It was exactly one month since Dad had collapsed on our bathroom floor. It was two weeks until my seventeenth birthday. My brother Ron was fifteen years old, Doug was fourteen, Karen was eleven and Jenny was just ten years old. She would be eleven in July marking eleven years of our family living in Washtucna. Mom was just three months shy of her fortieth birthday. Dad was dead. I couldn't comprehend it. It was like I was suddenly living in the worst dream ever.

I mentioned that I knew God personally. I had asked him into my life two years prior to this, and I was learning what it meant to respect God with the awe He deserved and yet come to Him with my own questions, concerns, and fears. My walk with God was young, but God was huge in my life already, and I saw Him working all around me. I had seen my father trust God when my grandfather died so suddenly and now I needed to do the same.

That Friday morning it was decided that my little sisters, Karen and Jenny, and youngest brother, Doug, would stay at home with Mom. My older brother, Ron, and I would go on the basketball road trip as planned, because he felt that was what Dad would want him to do, and Mom didn't want him to go alone. I took the cupcakes to school my grandmother had made for my sister's class to use at their Valentine's Day party. I maneuvered through the halls to my own classes receiving hugs from classmates and friends. Students and adults alike were in tears, some standing off as if they didn't want to make things worse for me by my seeing them cry. My body was trying to go about each moment of the day as usual, but my soul was in a fog. It was surreal and I felt God carrying me as I went along.

The next Monday, it seemed the whole town and a great deal many folks from surrounding towns came to my father's funeral. Our family sat in the pew at church we always sat in, second from the front on the right side of church, only Dad wasn't sitting there with us. The pastor's voice sounded like the grownups in a Charlie Brown movie, all mumbles and nothing that connected to me personally. Mom was brave, the rest of us cried off and on, and before I knew it we were all outside the church watching as they carried the casket to the hearse.

All my relatives and many friends got into cars for the three-hour ride to St. Maries, Idaho where Dad would be buried in a family plot near my grandfather. We had been at that exact spot in the cemetery only eight months earlier, in June. My dad had stood so tall beside my grandmother, supporting her throughout the graveside service. Now my sisters and brothers and I sat in the front row on folding chairs next to our mother, and with great sadness we watched as they lowered the rose covered casket into the ground. Being February, it was cold. Snow fell softly around us, but the outer cold couldn't compete with the ice cold reality I felt inside while sitting by my father's open grave. A little bit of me died that day, and a whole lot of me grew up. Life wasn't as I thought it would always be, and nothing could have prepared me for that realization.

I finished my junior year of high school, worked my summer job as usual, and began my last year of high school in Washtucna the next fall. I had planned to become a teacher like my father, something I had decided on many years prior when I used to help him set up his classroom at the beginning of the school year and put everything away again at the end of the year. I loved opening the boxes of the brand new text books and helping put up the new posters on the walls of his room. My dad loved teaching, and it showed, and he had inspired me to love it as well. I wanted to spend my life teaching school, just like he had always done. Because of that, I had begun to make plans to attend a nearby college and earn an Elementary Education degree.

Mommy and Angela, posing on her 1st birthday.

Angela, helping Daddy write a new song!

Angela, age 2, the strong-willed child finally asleep…
with her feet planted firmly on the floor!

Angela, patting newborn baby Josh's back.

Angela, age 3, playing her favorite song.

Angela, age 7, practicing her violin for baby brother, Bryan.

Our quiver is full!

Angela, performed the Zigeunerweisen, better known as the
Gypsy Airs, as a senior in high school with the Wenatchee Valley
Symphony as the winner of the Young Artist's Competition.

Angela and Erik's wedding day!

Angela, preparing for an upcoming concert.

Angela, at her 30th surprise birthday party, given to her by Erik.

Angela poses for a picture to be used on her business cards.

Angela, the accomplished violinist, in all her beauty.

Angela meets her relatives – May 1976. Back row:
Kathy, Great Grandpa Lloyd Rumelhart,
Front row: Great Grandma Agnes Esmay, Great Great Grandpa Ross
Rumelhart, Angela, 6 months old, Great Grandma Marie Rumelhart.

Grandma Agnes Esmay, Kathy Esmay, age 15, Grandpa Guy Esmay – 1968

The Esmay Family – 1967
Back row: Joanne and Don; Middle row: Kathy, Doug
and Ron; Front row: Karen and Jennifer

CHAPTER 8
My Mom

Unfortunately enough, soon after my father's death, our mother began to experience symptoms that prompted her to see her doctor. She had taken Dad's place in helping our grandmother with the ongoing legal details of Grandpa Esmay's will, as well as having to oversee the settling of Dad's will too. She was grieving, she was tired, and she had five children to continue to provide for. She thought she was just experiencing some form of exhaustion, so off to her doctor she finally went. After many tests, and trips back and forth to the out-of-town doctor's office, she was given a diagnosis of Leukemia, another type of cancer we knew very little about. She didn't seem to be very concerned and began a routine of traveling to Spokane for vaccine-like shots that were supposed to help her feel better. She didn't share much about her illness with us kids, and she seemed to be fine, capable of doing what she needed and wanted to do as long as she kept seeing her doctor. We were all grieving the loss of our father, and we knew she was as well, but in our daily conversations, communication about how we felt or how we were doing, were absent. We had the support of friends, and the routine of daily life, and we did the expected; we put one foot in front of the other and kept on going. Mom did the same.

By the time I finished high school and began college about an hour from home, Mom had become a part of a national leukemia research group that took her to Roswell Cancer Institute in Buffalo, New York a few times a year. There she became a guinea pig for the research being done with Leukemia, and she received medical attention for her own illness at the same time. Her parents would come to Washtucna to stay with my siblings whenever she had a trip, and I received updates at college from her regularly. This lifestyle became a new routine for our family, and again, we adjusted and were managing.

My first year of college was coming to a close and finals were the next week when I received a phone call from my Grandpa Rumelhart, my mom's father. Mom was in the hospital in Buffalo, New York and had been there much longer than ever before. Each Monday I received news that if her white blood count remained low she would be released to come home the next weekend. But come the end of the week the count would be too high, and she would be told she would need to stay a bit longer. This had happened several times already, and we were beginning to be worried. She had gone to Buffalo in early May, and should have been home by Mother's Day. My grandmother and sisters had baked a cake in anticipation of her arrival. Then the blood count went up, and Mom had to stay put. Back home they froze the cake saying they would just have Mother's Day later when she got home. Her birthday came, and went, the end of May as did my sister, Karen's, which was the day after Mom's. Grandma and my sisters had taken the cake out of the freezer at least once or twice with word of mom's coming home, only to be disappointed that she couldn't come.

When I got the phone call from my grandfather, he told me that the doctor in Buffalo felt that someone needed to go be with Mom to give her enough moral support to enable her to be flown to a hospital closer to home or she wouldn't make it. I had no idea she was that ill, and I was shocked. I came home that very day, and Grandma was so upset about me flying to Buffalo alone that she insisted I take another sibling with me. Mom was to know nothing about our coming until we walked into her room. The doctor had contacted a few of the nurses at the hospital that had befriended my mom during her year and a half worth of visits there, and they were going to meet us at the airport and let us stay in their homes while we visited our mother.

The next day a friend drove my littlest sister, Jenny, and me to the Spokane airport. From there we flew to Chicago, and on to Buffalo where perfect strangers greeted us with tears and hugs and extreme relief that we were there. Within a few hours of our arrival, we walked into our mother's hospital room completely unprepared to see the frail, ailing woman in the bed that was indeed our mother. Jenny was almost thirteen years old, and I was just nineteen. She was too young to realize the implications of what we saw, and I was just old enough to know I needed to hide it from her, and from my mom too. The doctor asked to talk with me alone, and I found myself in a room with a man I thought was going to cure my mother. Instead he told me that she was near death, that she had been receiving blood transfusions, and that they were all that were keeping her alive. He asked my blood type, which was the same as my mother's, and he made arrangements for me to give blood that would go directly to her. He said he hoped that would give her enough strength so she could be taken home and cared for further at the Spokane hospital, the very same one where my father had undergone brain surgery a little over two years before.

I gave blood. I stayed with my sister in the homes of our new friends from the hospital, and for about a week we spent the better part of each day sitting with our mother while she regained some strength. Evidently, the transfusions always gave her a boost of energy and helped bring her blood count down. As hoped for by the doctor, my donated blood proved to be doing just exactly that. Back home my grandparents were working out a plan with my mom's oldest brother for him to fly to Buffalo and accompany her to Spokane. My sister and I had done our part, we were told, and we were to fly home without her. Mom was very surprised when she first saw us in her room, and nervous about our having traveled so far to come see her. But as the days went by she was appreciative and excited to get home to the rest of her family. About a week after our arrival, Jenny and I hugged Mom goodbye and were whisked off to the airport to retrace our flight home and be greeted in Spokane by friends.

Jenny was taken home, and I went back to college to make up the finals I had missed the week before. I never paid attention to the grades I received for taking those tests, and I am not even sure to this day if they were ever sent to me back home. Once I finished the tests, I packed up my room and left for Washtucna. It was June, 1972, three years since my bus ride to California and the death of my Grandpa Esmay. I was living in a continual fog that just didn't seem to want to lift, and I was flying through it on autopilot.

Our mother's parents were exhausted and needed to return to their home after having been in our home for over a month. My siblings and I regrouped and began the summer as best we could, on our own. Because we lived in a small town surrounded by wheat farms, the summer work available to us as youths either had to do with a business in town or a farm out of town. That summer, like most summers before, both my brothers had jobs driving wheat trucks for farmers during harvest time. My sisters were babysitting in town for a family I had once worked for, and I was working for the family of another wheat farmer. My brothers stayed on their farms all week long, and I went back and forth from mine daily. We were home together on Saturdays, and on Sundays after church, we all packed into our family's car, and drove the hour and a half to Spokane to visit our mother.

Amazingly enough, moving nearer to home had indeed helped Mom get better. Each Sunday we spent as much time as we could with her, sometimes taking walks with her in the hallway outside her room. If she needed something, we brought it from home or went to downtown Spokane and got it for her. Her parents visited her during the week, and we made our weekend pilgrimage, and it all seemed to be helping her, with the promise that one of these days, she would be well enough to come home herself. The upside was she was being treated with chemotherapy, which was new for her, and it seemed to be helping her greatly. The downside was she was losing her hair so we got her some wigs. She was seeing her children weekly, and she adapted to the changes in her life with great appreciation and dignity. A new normal set in for our family, and summertime continued on.

One of the first times we went to see Mom, she had asked me to bring her checkbook, and some other papers from home. Now that our grandparents weren't living with us, she needed me to pay some bills and take care of things she couldn't do from her hospital room. I remember being amazed that she was willing to trust me with this responsibility. I didn't mind, but I knew it was something she had always done, even when Dad was alive, and it felt so odd knowing she was passing the job onto me. We had grown up in a community where boys in junior high learned to drive wheat trucks and tractors with their dads, and girls helped cook harvest meals and oversaw the care of young children when they were still young themselves. I had been babysitting for families all over town since I was in sixth grade. My little sisters and brother, Doug, shared a paper route for years. My brother, Ron, worked at the meat market after school to earn extra money as a high school student. Ron and Doug had been doing all the outdoor chores Dad had always done since his death. We were all used to learning new skills, and doing our fair share of work, so having my mom hand me the financial responsibility for our family wasn't something I couldn't handle, it just meant she wasn't handling it anymore, and that was a jolt.

The middle of July we took a cake and candles to the hospital to celebrate our youngest sister, Jenny's, thirteenth birthday. Mom wasn't feeling well enough to get out of bed, so we had the party right there in her room. We had all taken our birthday gifts for Jen with us, and mom had called with suggestions of things to purchase for her ahead of time so she had something for her too. We tried to have a good time, but it all felt so strange.

One morning, a few weeks after Jen's birthday, I received, yet again, another phone call from Grandpa Rumelhart. It was early morning, and I was preparing to drive to my job on the farm where I worked. My grandfather was in tears. He told me I needed to hurry, that they needed me at the hospital as soon as possible. He and Grandma were there with my mom, and she wasn't doing well at all that day. My siblings were already at their jobs that morning, so I left immediately for Spokane, leaving a note for my sisters saying I would call them when I knew what else we needed to do. I knew the moment I saw my mom that she was trying so hard to hang on to life, but that she was also quite ready to let go of it. I sat with Mom, and I talked with her doctor who said they had done all they could for her. I hugged my grandparents who were in such pain as they watched their only daughter slipping away. Mom wasn't able to speak much, and she slept often. Some time went by, and I just sat with her. Grandma and Grandpa were taking turns making phone calls to family members on the phone out in the hallway. A friend came by to visit Mom, not knowing what was happening, so I spoke with the woman outside of Mom's room. She wanted so badly to see my mother. She was in tears. I woke Mom up and told her she had a visitor, but she said no, she didn't want to see anyone…except her kids. I sent the woman away and called my pastor and asked him to please hurry and gather my siblings and get them to the hospital as soon as he could. He assured me he would do so. I knew the ninety-mile drive from Washtucna to Spokane, coupled with the time it would take to gather my siblings, would be at least a few hours. I prayed it would be soon enough.

Before long, we were all there, jammed into that small hospital room again. Grandma and Grandpa stepped out into the hall trying to hide their tears. I motioned for my brothers and sisters to come closer to the bed, and I woke Mom up. She couldn't speak. She just looked slowly, and longingly, at each of the faces of her five children as they looked at her. No one spoke, there was no sound. It was as if time was frozen for the moment, and then she laid back into her pillow. I motioned for each person to come, and give her a kiss, and they did. Then they went into the hallway. Grandma and Grandpa took my sisters and brothers home with them that night. My pastor and I sat beside my mom on either side, holding her hands all night long. From time to time she would open her eyes, and move as if she had been shaken, and then she would look at the crucifix on the wall at the foot of her bed, and relax, and close her eyes again. We were not Catholic, but I have always been grateful for that cross in her room in that Catholic hospital that night. Eventually, I dozed with my head on the bed beside her hand. Miraculously, Mom made it through the night. As morning came, so did an uninformed medical technician who entered the room to give Mom a breathing treatment. Funny, no one else had come into the room since my siblings and grandparents had left, but standing there with a cheery smile was this young man just wanting to do his job, and I bit his head off. At first I tried to tell him quietly that she was too weak to do the treatment, but he was insistent. My pastor had left the room to get a nurse, and I finally told the man quite sternly to LEAVE THE ROOM. He did, and the doctor came in as he went out. The doctor asked me and my pastor to leave for a minute. We did, and when we came back Mom was gone. I rushed to her bed and called her name and hugged her tightly. Both the doctor and my pastor pulled me off of her, and in a moment I gained control of myself. The doctor placed the sheet over her head and took me into another room. He explained what would happen next, and to this day I have no idea what he said. When I went back into her room, Mom and her bed were gone. I was instructed to gather her things from her closet. I was nineteen years old, and I did as I was told.

The next thing that I remember is that I was the one entering the kitchen at my grandparents' house. I told them Mom was gone, and I found each of my brothers and sisters and told them what had happened. My youngest sister, Jenny, was out in the backyard with our grandfather looking at his prize flower beds. As I came around the corner to find them, Grandpa burst into tears and left Jen and me alone. I approached her and held her as I told her Mom was gone. She asked me if she had been in pain, and I said no, that she had slipped from sleep to heaven in an instant. Then Jenny asked if Mom was with Dad, and I hugged Jen and said, yes, they were in heaven together. She looked at me and said, "Then that is what we wanted, right?" I hugged her hard, and told her yes, and that I knew that God had a plan for us, and that he would take care of us kids now. With that we entered the house with everyone else, and the day went by.

A few days later I sat with my grandparents and my sisters and brothers in those same folding chairs beside our mother's open grave. This was the third time we had been there in three years. Just two and a half years earlier we sat in freezing cold weather in our Sunday clothes, and nothing could keep out the cold. This time we sat again in our Sunday best, and the hot August sun caused us to sweat, yet I remember feeling chilled. Again, we placed roses on the top of the casket, and again, we watched as it was lowered into the ground. There were tears and hugs, and then it was over, and my siblings and I were back at home, in our house, alone, without a reason to drive to the hospital the next Sunday.

I chose not to return to college the month after Mom died. Instead I remained at home with my siblings as we pieced our lives back together over the next year. During my first year of college I had met Gordon Schuster, who ended up being the man of my dreams. Our relationship continued to grow after Mom's death, even though I was home keeping house for my siblings, and he was back at college working on his Master's program. At the end of the school year he and I married, and we spent our first three months of marriage with my siblings in Washtucna, as we all prepared for the next stage in our lives.

My new mother and father-in-law offered to have my sisters come live with them on their farm outside of St. John. My husband had been offered a job across the state in Bellevue. My sisters weren't excited about moving to St. John at first, but neither did they want to move to the big city with us, after being raised in a small town. My oldest brother, Ron, had just graduated from high school and was accepted into a college, also out of town. Doug had been befriended by a family who had recently lost their father suddenly, and he was very comfortable settling in with them and remaining in Washtucna for his senior year of high school.

Looking back, the changes we made that next summer after losing our mom probably came too quickly, but it seemed at the time to be for the best for everyone involved. We loved our home and the memories we had there, but it was not easy living where it felt like Mom or Dad could come walking around the corner at any minute. The people in town evidently trusted us to care for ourselves, for they did not interfere at all, but watched from afar. This made it a bit like living in a glass house. After all, here we were, five kids under the age of twenty, living completely by ourselves. I had gone to our lawyer following Mom's death to complete paperwork needed to close her will, and to make sure that Dad's was finalized too. The lawyer went to great lengths to convince me that we all needed to be living with relatives or someone else since I was not yet twenty years of age. I told him that was not going to happen. So he followed through on the paperwork Mom had drawn up previously with him during her illness. She had decided that I would be the guardian of my siblings until they each became twenty-one years of age or married. The lawyer said he hoped it would work. It did. Mom had also added my name to her bank account so I was able to use her savings and the money our family received from our parents' wills to keep us financially stable. During the year while living with my siblings again, I even paid off our home purchased by our folks some fourteen years earlier there in Washtucna.

Finally, the day came when everything we owned was divided up, and packed, and ready to be moved, along with each person, to new beginnings. It is never easy to start over, and to say now that it all went smoothly back then would be another way of sweeping some of life's challenges under the rug of our hearts. It was very difficult, but looking back we all know now, it is what saved us.

I think it is a miracle that none of my siblings and I have lost our minds, completely at least. And that none of us have jumped off a bridge or become addicted to something to take the sting of life away. Instead we have all grown up, stretching as we went, and, yes, probably stuffing a great deal of what happened to us deep down into our souls. We have met the loves of our lives, married, and raised our children. And we have remained true to the faith our parents raised us to believe. Our God has been our balm and our comfort. He has guided our lives and allowed us to laugh, and love, and live as we should. As siblings we have kept close in heart, if not always close in contact, and to this day we are blessed to have each other in our lives.

As I write this chapter it has been forty-five years now since the death of our father, and forty-three years since the death of our mother. Dad was forty-five when he died and Mom was just forty-two. We have all outlived our parents by almost twenty years. It is nearly impossible to imagine them in their nineties, but that is how old they would be today. All of our grandparents are gone now too, along with a great many of our aunts and uncles. Yet the Esmay family has grown by leaps and bounds. If our parents were still alive today they would have eighteen grandchildren, and thirteen great-grandchildren, with two more on the way. They have missed nineteen weddings, including all five of ours, and we have missed having them there at the birth of each of our children. We know we will see them again, and each one of us is blessed with that promise. We know there will be a huge family reunion in heaven someday for us all. Until then, I believe we have lived our lives in a manner that exemplifies the values our parents set before us. I know that their love has remained a stabilizing factor in my life, and the lives of everyone in our family.

The last few chapters have come from places in my heart that have been locked away for years. My brain has struggled as memories have escaped from it and have been formulated into words on paper. The day my friend first prompted me to consider that the grief I was experiencing upon Angela's death, was layered grief, I had no idea what exactly that meant. I still have much to learn about it, even though it has been almost eight years now since Angela died. But I believe I have journeyed further than ever possible by revisiting my past and the grief my soul suffered there.

Everyone is different. Each person's loss is incredibly personal, and everyone maneuvers through their own grief in their own way, even within families where the reason for the grief is the same. I am a product of my life, of the triumphs I have experienced as well as the trials. The people in my life and the blessings I have enjoyed because of them have also helped shape me into the person I am today. I have created my own stumbling blocks, for sure, and have taken many detours I probably could and should have ignored. But, I am here. I am alive. I am living, and I am growing past the grief that has threatened to paralyze my life so many times. God has preserved me, protected me, and promised me a life everlasting. Because of that, joy will come in the morning, and one day every moment of grief I have endured will be gone, and in its place will be an eternity of time with those I have missed so very much. I wait for that day with anticipation. I cannot explain it in words. But I know grief and loss will not always be a part of my life. Hallelujah!

CHAPTER 9

The Importance of Family Time

When my siblings and I began living our lives away from one another after the death of our mother, it was important for us to stay in contact with each other. But it wasn't easy. We all lived several hours apart, and we each became very busy with our own lives. At Christmas time we gathered at my husband's parent's farm where my sisters were living. Ron came from college and Doug came from Washtucna where he was finishing high school. My father and mother-in-law treated us all as family and loved having us come together with them for the holidays. This became a pattern for several Christmases and on other occasions as well. As time went on and my sisters graduated from high school, each one came to live with Gordon and me while they prepared for their careers and life on their own. My brothers had the opportunity to be at the same college for a time and shared life together during those years. Eventually, though, each of my siblings began their careers, married, and settled into their own lives and started their own families. We were each blessed to have very supportive spouses, and loving in-laws, and for that we were very grateful. Holidays were spent with our own individual families, often times in the company of our in-laws. We did visit one another as we could throughout the year, and for a time four out of five of us were living near one another in the Spokane area. For many years, it was a matter of driving within the state of Washington to stay in touch, and that was a huge blessing. During the five years that Gordon and I lived in Indiana, special family occasions such as weddings brought us and our children from our home to our families back in Washington so we could celebrate together. After Gordon and I moved from Indiana back to Central Washington, we started a new tradition.

Karen and her family were living on the west side of the state, and everyone else still lived on the east side in Spokane. So, we came up with the idea of coming together at our house, in the middle of the state, for Thanksgiving. Whoever could come came, and my siblings and I filled our home to the brim with our young children and each other. What fun it was to watch each other's children growing up. We enjoyed meals together and creating traditions for the children. One such favorite was making gingerbread houses from graham crackers and frosting, complete with every kind of cookie and candy you can imagine. The kids also drew names at Thanksgiving for a Christmas gift exchange later. The highlight was nighttime when all the children crawled into their sleeping bags in the living room filling the house with their giggles and promises to go to sleep quickly! During the summers we sisters exchanged kids for a week or so, and the cousins spent time together at church camps or on family outings. We met for vacation time together as we could and for special birthdays. We gathered for our grandparents' fiftieth wedding anniversary, and for their special birthdays, and eventually for their funerals. Time stands still for no one, and it didn't stand still for the Esmay family either.

Before we knew it, the little children in our families were grown enough to have jobs of their own and to head off to college. Then it became difficult to gather our families together during the holidays. For the next season of life, we siblings saw each other at the high school graduations of our children, and before we knew it, at their weddings. Visits took place with one family seeing another, but rarely were we all together at any one time. Life remained so for many years.

During the fall of 2006 Jenny began to pester Karen and me about getting our families together again over Thanksgiving. Her children were the youngest of all of our five families, and she didn't want them to miss out on knowing their cousins, and the rest of us. I tried to explain to her that it wasn't easy to get my own four kids and their spouses together for any holiday, and that it hadn't worked for Thanksgiving for many years. Jen was relentless. She said she feared that if we didn't make an effort to get together for fun at least once a year, then we would find ourselves seeing each other only at weddings and funerals. So I promised her I would think about it and see what I could do. But, it just wasn't going to work that Thanksgiving.

Soon after, Gordon and I were blessed when all of our own children, and their spouses, gathered at our house over the New Year's weekend, since we weren't able to be together for Christmas. We had such a good time saying goodbye to 2006 and hello to 2007 together. During dinner the last night of our visit, I tossed the idea of a huge Esmay family reunion out to everyone. After some discussion and total support, we all decided it would only work if we did it during the summertime instead of during the winter holidays. A few days after everyone had headed home from our house, I sent a letter to my siblings saying that we needed to have a family reunion, and I suggested that we choose a weekend in July to make it happen. I mentioned in my letter that Jen was right, and if we didn't begin gathering just for fun, we would eventually be seeing each other only at weddings and funerals. The response was a unanimous yes, and Jen was thrilled! By the end of January, the first ever "Esmay Family Reunion" was scheduled to happen at our house the third weekend of July, just about five months away! The Esmay family had grown to about thirty-six of us, and it had been years since we had all been together. It was about time, and there was nothing but enthusiasm as plans were made for the new anticipated event.

Then the unthinkable happened, and only a little over two weeks after we put the date for the reunion on our calendars, Angela was suddenly taken from us. As per Jen's prediction as many family members as could came together at our church, and then at the cemetery for the services to celebrate Angela's life. Angela had been so excited about coming to the family reunion, and I guess in a way, she brought our hearts together for the first family gathering in a long, long time. It would fortunately not be the last.

That July, all of my brothers and sisters came with many of their children to be with Gordon and me and our family for our first official "Family Reunion." We began on Friday with dinner and a time of sharing about our lives while we ate bowls full of popcorn and candy and played a family quiz game. People put up tents in our backyard and slept all over our house in sleeping bags. Saturday we headed to the river using my sister's boat and picnicked to our hearts content. Afterwards, we fired up the grill at our house for another dinner, and we watched old family movies together. We ended the day around the fire pit for s'mores and conversation late into the night. Sunday we gathered at the cemetery to remember Angela and placed flowers on her grave. People prayed, and through tears we sang a song from her memorial service. After lunchtime we took pictures to commemorate the weekend, and then everyone headed home. Gordon and I were exhausted, but it was a good exhaustion, and we knew we had experienced something special, and very much needed.

As I write this chapter, this summer will mark the ninth Esmay family reunion, and we look forward to it with great zeal. No year has been the same, and not everyone has been able to come every year, but the reunions continue to be a source of fun and relaxation, and a time of catching up and bonding for our entire family. Now when we gather for weddings or for funerals, at least we also know that we have a special time planned in the summer to be together just for fun.

I am a party planner, and my family has graciously allowed me to be the organizer behind each year's reunion. We have a set theme and have enjoyed decorating to match it as well as dressing as best we can to embellish the weekend extravaganza. We plan the menu and backyard game competition around the theme and everyone has a hand in making the weekend successful. We dressed as cowboys for the "Country Cowboy" year and learned to line dance outside. We purchased flowered leis and wore flowered shirts for the "Hawaiian" year, and, yes, we learned to hula too. Thank goodness our back yard has a rather high fence so the neighbors can't see what all we do! I used ideas from my old Girl Scout book for the "Survival of the Fittest" year. And we even had "Christmas in July" one year when Gordon helped me put up all our Christmas decorations. We thoroughly enjoyed a snowman making competition where teams had to wrap someone up with toilet paper to make them into a snowman. We followed that with a Christmas white elephant gift exchange, and the traditional "ugly Christmas sweater" contest. The year after that, the theme was "Happy Birthday," and we threw a gigantic birthday party for everyone all weekend long. And last year we let each family represent their favorite college sports team, and we played a rip-roaring game of Family Feud as we competed as Ducks, Cougars, and Huskies! Now you know the college teams we like best! We have persevered through rainy weekends and those when the temperatures reached one hundred degrees. Last year, with only two days-notice we had to move the entire event from our house in Wenatchee to my sister's house in Kent, due to the terrible smoke in our valley from the many fires in our area at the time. There were only adults and teenagers the first four years we gathered together, and since then we have added precious grandbabies to the mix. My siblings and I couldn't be happier! From baked ham and turkey, to fondue and burgers, we have done it all and loved every bit and bite of it. We don't see the reunions stopping any time soon, and all I can say is that if your family isn't getting together for a reunion once in a while, you ought to organize one. It is priceless!

Aside from the benefits of just enjoying our families, and having a terrific time together, the family reunions have played a huge part in the grief healing for all of us. Two years after our first reunion, we lost another family member, my brother, Ron's, son, Shane, died of cancer. He was only a few years older than Angela. They had walked together down the aisle at our brother, Doug's, wedding when they were mere youngsters. Nothing can take the place of Angela and Shane in our lives. But knowing how much they were loved by their families and being able to gather all together as one, occasionally, has been such a blessing, and a help. The hugs, the talks, the girl-time, and guy-times all of it, has been balm for our grieving hearts and encouragement for our futures together. I will always be glad that God prompted Jen to pull our family together purposely again. And as I write this, I am looking forward to pinpointing this year's reunion theme and getting the planning going with only five months to go!

CHAPTER 10

Carrying Angela with Me

In a few days my family and I will celebrate the eighth year anniversary of Angela's death. I say "celebrate" because I don't know what else to call the marking of a day in time that so changed our lives forever. Each year has been different. We have done different things to set apart the day, and in so doing, not be drawn backwards by it quite so very much. Through the years we have exchanged flowers with one another, called each other, and written our sentiments for all to read on some such media extension of ourselves. One year I had one of Angela's pictures printed on a postcard with a little information about her and about the collision on the back. We passed them out to people who wanted one. We encouraged everyone to give them to someone along with a free cup of coffee or some other gift of kindness in honor of all the kindnesses Angela did for people when she was alive. Each year Gordon and I placed flowers on our daughter's grave, and we spend a bit of time sitting under her tree beside it, thinking, and wondering still, just how it all came to be real.

February 11th is one of those days when we want to shout to the whole world, and ask everyone to stop what they are doing, and think for a moment about the beautiful women whose lives and families were changed forever that fateful night. We will remember with aching hearts, and great love, Angela and Kjersten. And we will continue to reach out to their friend, Kelly, who survived the crash, and let her know that our love for her is strong, and that we are grateful that she is living her life to the fullest, just as her two friends would want her to do. We shall forever share in the message of not drinking when you drive as a way of preventing anyone else from dying from, or living through, the horror our families have experienced.

As we approached that eighth year, my husband and I were participating in a small group Bible study from church. We had just begun a ten week study on suffering, focusing on how God used suffering in our lives. Everybody had the opportunity to share about the suffering they had experienced and how that had played out in their life. Many of us in the group were able to relate to suffering that comes from the loss of one or both parents, or the loss of a job and financial security, or the loss of friends, and the changes that come in life as time marches on. But Gordon and I were the only people present who had experienced the loss of a child, and we were encouraged to share from our hearts, and our lives, our feelings about that specific kind of suffering.

Over a period of weeks, we shared much about how the loss took place and about who Angela was as a person, and as our daughter, and how we have journeyed through the absence of having her in our lives. Our group listened with great empathy and aching hearts to whatever we said as we shared from time to time throughout the weeks of our study. As a whole, our group came to the understanding that any and all loss that cuts deep into one's heart and life is suffering, and that the pain experienced is the great equalizer as far as suffering is concerned. There is no need for comparison. Pain is pain, and to the person experiencing it, it is all-encompassing. Our group was able to appreciate the depth of each person's story, and together look past the story to our heavenly Father who walked with each of us as we journeyed through the sufferings experienced in our lives. We were able to focus on the truth that God is in control even when we feel everything is out of control, and that He has a plan even when we think our plans are thwarted.

We came to understand that God can use all suffering that comes our way to not only strengthen us personally, but also to strengthen our relationship with him. We were reminded in our study that pain, and loss, and suffering comes to every person that has ever lived, given enough time on this earth. With that premise we came to the conclusion that our response to such pain, and loss, and suffering is what causes us to be beaten down by it in defeat or to rise above it in victory. We all agreed that God's involvement in our lives had indeed enabled each of us to rise above the battles suffering had brought to us thus far in life. What a blessing it was to grow through this particular study together and come out on the other side, linked arm in arm with others who have stood toe to toe with great suffering, and who have continued to stand upright in spite of it. The timing was perfect for Gordon and me as we took what we had learned into the eighth year of our loss of Angela.

I have encountered many people over the past eight years who have sincerely wanted to understand how I have personally "made it through" losing my daughter. In attempting to share my thoughts and feelings for a friend once, I came to a better understanding myself of just what has transpired through my grief journey, and what it has done to me. I have already mentioned early on that grief is physical, mental, and emotional for sure, as well as spiritual. Grief is also very, very personal. I am a very visual person when it comes to my thoughts and experiences. So much of the processing of my grief has happened in my mind and my heart in full Technicolor.

In particular, as stated earlier, I had a very difficult time getting past the collision scene itself, as that had become imprinted in my mind and heart shortly after Angela's death. But that hasn't been my only challenge. God has creatively used some amazing analogies to nudge me through the difficulties I have had along the way. As I was writing for my friend trying to explain what my grief journey has been like, one of those analogies formulated in my mind…in full color, and I had to share it with her. The following is an attempt to explain it to you.

When I first learned of Angela's death there was, of course, great shock as I maneuvered through the first few weeks. Very soon, the memorial services were done, and we had to return home and start to live without her. I struggled to do that. I could not figure out how to live without being able to call her, or listen to her voice, or just know that she was doing what she always did, day to day, as she went about living her life, before it all changed. As the shock of it all began to wear off, the pain and emptiness sank in, and the silence became deafening.

What I ended up doing was to metaphorically wrap Angela's broken body in my grief quilt and cradle her there as I first sat in the depths of my loss. Eventually, I stood up and proceeded to move forward, carrying her in my arms in front of me as I attempted to get back into life. I think that is why I was so unable to focus on anything or any task at hand. My hands were full as she lay across them, and all I could see was her lifeless body out in front of me. Nothing else took my attention from her.

Because I had already experienced the loss of my grandfather and both parents, when Angela died, I knew what it was like to lose someone in death. I knew that in time I would no longer hear their voice in my head, or imagine the details of their personality that so reminded me of them. I knew that time would carry me past the empty space left by that person I loved so much. I knew that eventually memories would fade or become condensed to places in my mind that held them so I could come back to them, like photo albums, from time to time, when I had time, or when a date on the calendar caused me to remember them. I knew that the passage of time could allow me to forget the negative, and perhaps even exaggerate the positive, about the person I knew so well. I understood that even though our lives were once so entwined together, I would be forced to continue to live the rest of my life separate from their connection to me. Yes, I would be able to keep the influence and contribution these loved ones made to not only my life, but to who I am as a person. But mostly, I knew that in all certainty they would become less and less a part of me, and I would become more and more of the person I would grow into, over time, without them. As the years would go by, I knew there would be more forgetting than there would be remembering. That especially terrified me when it came to Angela. I did not want to forget her or live without her being such a huge part of my life, and I definitely did not want to lose her in any way, shape, or form.

And so I carried her in my arms with me wherever I went. As time went by, and I had to keep moving forward in my own life, I managed to shift her weight, and I held her with one arm only. I was able to semi-focus on my job, my family, and whatever I had to do, with one arm free. For brief moments, throughout the day, I did what I needed to do without focusing on her. She was beside me, not in front of me, and I became comfortable with that. After months of carrying her around like this, I shifted her again, and pushed her up onto my back. With both hands free, I could do more and be more involved in life. I was able to laugh and be happy a little bit, and yet there was great comfort in feeling her close against me, and it seemed like she wasn't really gone altogether.

I carried Angela on my back into the first year anniversary, and then into the trial that began three months later against the drunk driver who had taken her life. During the most difficult of moments, I am sure I pulled her back into my arms, and then finally, as things settled down, I shifted her around to my back again. I was learning to participate in life and at least look and act like things were getting back to normal. But carrying someone on your back brings its own kind of pain and certainly isn't normal at all. I am sure my family and closest friends could tell that I was still burdened under the weight of my grief. For me, this stage of grief lasted a long, long while, and even though I was growing in my understanding of grief, and my trust in God to carry me through it, I was still just plodding along.

There is no specific time that I can pinpoint when Angela slipped from her position on my back into my heart, but I know that is what happened. Perhaps it came four years in, with the birth of my first grandchild, or year six, with the last wedding in our family. Or maybe it was something else along the way that allowed the joy of living to overtake the sadness of loss. I found that joy certainly did increase as I became more fully engaged in the lives of my family who were living right in front of me. I can't explain it, but I know that Angela is tucked into my heart where she will always stay. Her radiance and enthusiasm for everything she did and everyone she knew is tucked in there with her. I can spend time with her there and momentarily be completely immersed in her laughter or a conversation we once had or a memory of her doing something I loved watching her do. But because she is there, tucked safely in my heart, I am also free to live my life as fully as possible without the heavy anchors of grief pulling me down.

Having to live through the death of my daughter has been my worst nightmare. The same would have been true if it had been any one of my other children, not just Angela. I have heard it said that the closest a woman will come to her own death without dying, is when she is birthing her children. Somehow, the act of delivering a child, and the pain experienced during that physical process brings a woman very close to the brink of losing her own life. I have heard that, but I disagree. For me at least, the death of my child caused me to die, in more ways than I can put into print. When it first happened, I would not have believed anyone if they had told me that one day that feeling of being dead would be replaced by feeling fully alive again- that one day I would feel contentment, and happiness, and joy in my life. I wouldn't have believed it, but it is true. It has happened for me.

I know now that I cannot lose Angela. As long as my mind can remember, I will remember her. I will always love her, for she became a part of me, not just an influence for the person I have become, but a real part of me. And I know, for a fact, that I will be with her again, in heaven, just as I will be with my mother, my father, my grandparents, and the rest of my immediate family one day. For I am one of those very fortunate mothers whose children have all believed in God, who have put their trust in God, and who will be preserved eternally by God. Nothing matters more to me than that! I pray the same will be true for each of my dear grandchildren, as their loving parents raise them with an understanding of the God who loves them so very much.

Recently I heard the testimony of a mother and father who lost their daughter as a newborn child. My heart went out to them as I listened to how they suffered through their grief and came out on the other side of it. One specific statement caught my attention as the mother shared how she went from days spent in bed paralyzed by her grief, to finally being up and involved in the life of her family, and then as time passed, coming to the place where she could experience a joy-filled life once again. She said it was a ten year journey. Wow! As I heard her say that I could understand and agree that it takes a great deal of time to grow through all the stages of grief, and to become transformed by the process, and come out successfully on the other side. I could relate to that, but when she said it took about ten years, I sighed. Perhaps she is right. It just might take two more years of moving forward, before I am more fully free of the claws of grief.

It is true that you don't ever get over the loss of a child or a parent or a spouse or a friend…but you do get through it. And getting through it takes hard work, lots of time, and acceptance that the process is happening even when you don't think you are moving at all. My experience leads me to believe that it isn't so much about moving through one's grief as it is about allowing grief to move through you. A person has the choice, and the ability to keep the grief from moving at all, and to become stuck in one stage or place with it. And it is possible to shut the door on grief altogether and cause it to become stuffed deep down into your heart and your soul, far away from your mind and your emotions. But that grief will eventually leak out, or worse, implode or explode its way through your life, and the damage done will be immense. If I have learned anything at all about grief, it is that it is best to let it happen naturally, and to move with it, and at the same time, to keep one's eyes on the promise that grief is indeed for the night, and that joy comes in the morning. It is so very hard to believe that in the beginning, but there is life after grief. The challenge is to get there through a healthy process. In my humble opinion, that happens best with the understanding that you are not alone on your journey, and that those who love you and care about you are supporting you in so many ways. God was the captain of my support group, and he was the only one who could understand the depths of the pain I felt because he saw it within me. But I am so thankful for my husband, and my other children, and the friends who cared about me and prayed for me during the past long years. I hope that my prayers have been as helpful to my family as theirs have been to me. Together we will continue our journey in life as we live without Angela on this earth, and as we think about her entrance into her heavenly home. I know that each one of us looks forward to hugging her one day and to never having to be apart from her again.

CHAPTER 11
The Tenth Year Commemoration

Two more years have indeed gone by since Gordon and I began our eighth year of life after losing Angela. The summer prior to the actual tenth year anniversary of her passing, we began to think about how we would get through that momentous day. We talked about traveling to her hometown, and then on to Eugene, Oregon to take in a symphony concert where she last performed, but alas, there was no concert scheduled for around that date. We considered taking a trip somewhere so we could sit on a beach and soak in the sunshine while we tried to soak in the revelation that a full decade had passed since our last conversation with our daughter. Nothing we came up with doing seemed right until we thought about bringing all three of our children, their spouses and our grandchildren home to be with us. That seemed right. We weren't sure it was possible, but it did seem right.

The anniversary date was Saturday, February 11, 2017. It promised to be the middle of winter in our area of the world. Our daughter and her family lived in town near us, so it wasn't such an impossible task for them to set aside a full week to be together. But we would be asking our sons to interrupt their schedules, and travel with their families from Idaho and Tennessee, respectfully, to join us. We weren't sure they could do so even if they wanted to. Gordon and I prayed about it, thought about it, and finally asked everyone in our immediate family if they would consider coming home to commemorate the tenth year anniversary of Angela's entrance into heaven. The response was an immediate and unanimous YES! And so we began the plans for spending a week together the next February.

We decided early on that we didn't want this family time to be somber or overly emotional, even though we all knew we were coming together to mark a day that had been life-changing and sad for us all. We told everyone that we wanted to focus on all the good things that had happened in the life of our family over the past decade of time. This idea was met with great enthusiasm and relief as we all looked forward to being together.

Gordon and I elected to do some much-needed remodeling in our home prior to our family event so we threw ourselves into that project and rolled up our sleeves to get it all done in time. Somehow it helped to be painting walls, putting in new flooring, and moving furniture a number of times to accomplish everything we were trying to do. We wanted to surprise our kids and enjoy the finished space with them in it. It had been some time since our family had been all together in our home, and we wanted to make the best of it. As most home improvement projects go, we finished a few days after the necessary timeline, but it was just in time for our big event.

As feared, the winter weather threw a damper on things causing our Idaho family to double their driving time in snowy conditions to make it to our house. Our Tennessee gang ended up spending an unexpected two days and nights in Seattle waiting for the weather to let up so they could either fly or drive the last three hours to our home. Finally, with great relief and anticipation we were all under the same roof. Due to the change in travel time and weather, we had four days and three nights together instead of nearly a week, but we didn't care. We were all home!

Valentine's Day took place the week after our get-together, along with a birthday in our family, so being the party planner that I am, we celebrated each event the first two nights at dinnertime. We had a surprise birthday party the first night with a ham dinner complete with birthday cake and birthday gifts. The next night we enjoyed a turkey dinner with all the trimmings and Valentine candy treat bags for everyone. The third night we ate leftovers as we hurried to make time for a professional photographer to capture our first ever family portrait. He even took pictures of each family separately and gave us the proofs saying, "Do whatever you want with these!" I later made a photo book for each of our families to remember our time together, along with a large wall print of our family portrait. We are so glad we took time for pictures!

But the most meaningful time that we spent together was during the evening of February 11, the actual date of the tenth anniversary of losing our Angela. The grandchildren went to bed early, and the rest of us sat around the table as we all shared what had been going on in our lives over the past ten years including the most recent of days. Gordon asked our kids and their spouses to say whatever they wanted to say, but not to feel pressure to say anything at all. We weren't sure what would happen. What did happen will continue to be one of the most precious times in our lives for Gordon and me, as we listened to our family share from their hearts what it was like for each of them when Angela died. We heard things we had never heard before. There was laughter and some tears as our hearts were intertwined by the event that had so changed our lives a decade ago. Every single person, even those who hadn't been a part of our family back then, shared how they had grown through the process of grieving our universal loss. They talked about how God had carried them through the pain and heartache, and how he had even united them with their spouses in their grief. By the end of the evening our individual grief blended together and we gathered up the joy we jointly shared as a family. We were able to thank God for the blessing of seeing us all through the trial that could have so easily torn us apart. We prayed for each other's future needs and ambitions and also paid tribute to our dear Angela as we shared our memories of her. It was an evening that can never be repeated, but that will always be recalled as one of the most meaningful to Gordon and me.

The next day Bryan and his family headed to the airport for the journey back to Tennessee. It was hard to let them go, but we were so thankful for their coming to be with us. A few days later, Josh and his wife packed up and drove back home to Idaho, in better weather than they had come in. We were so grateful for their willingness to travel in such conditions to participate with us all. We all went back to our schedule and lives but we did so with our hearts full of love and gratitude for the family God had given to us. Gordon and I felt so thankful for the precious time our family had shared together. We were so glad we had taken time to commemorate the fact that we have one family member in heaven that will never be forgotten, and will always to be remembered, and loved. Together we had thanked God for giving Angela to us, and for all that she meant, and will continue to mean to our family. It was the best way we could have ever celebrated her life and the fact that her death was not the end of who she is to us.

I have not written much about Angela's husband, Erik Svendsen. When he and Angela married he truly became a part of our family, and after Angela died, we once told him we feared we would lose him over time as well. For we knew his life would need to move forward, the same as ours would, and as young as he was at the time of Angela's death, we figured he would one day quite possibly remarry and become a son-in-law to another family. Early on in our grief he assured us he wasn't going anywhere. How we appreciated his love, and concern for us, and the tremendous gift he gave to us from the moment we heard our daughter was gone. He supported us having her first memorial service in our home church where so many people who had known Angela from her youth could come and help us celebrate her life. He organized and led the second memorial service held at a school near where he and Angela lived so that her many violin students, and their families, and all of Angela's and Erik's friends could come and participate in celebrating her life close to where she had lived it. He sat with us as family at the church and at the graveside service where she was laid to rest, also in our hometown. He was pleased with the memorial stone we chose to use to mark her grave. In every way possible, Erik always shared Angela with us, in her life, and in her death. He checked in with us to see how we were doing in our grief, and we checked in with him. Only a few weeks after the services were over and we were supposed to be getting back to our normal lives, Erik and I had a phone conversation. We talked about how our lives would never really be normal again, and about how much it hurt to be in the very deepest part of our grief. He told me something that I will never forget. He said that even though we had no choice in our loss of Angela, and in the grief we felt for her, we still had the choice in "how" we would grieve. He told me that he had decided that he didn't want to just go through grief, but that he was determined to grow through his grief. I had not heard it stated that way before, and that day, on the phone, I told him I wanted to do the same thing. I am proud to say, Angela, you chose well, and your husband honored you by refusing to let grief destroy the love he had for you, and the person he was for you. He set up a scholarship program that would support, encourage, and enable young musicians to further their training as they auditioned for an annual scholarship award in Angela's name. She would have loved that! To this day, young musicians come together every spring to perform for the audition, and one person becomes the recipient of that year's monetary award. How we love hearing about the winner each year, and how we appreciate that Erik still oversees this project. As time moved on Erik found a wonderful woman he fell in love with, and he married her with our blessing, not that he needed it. We are so very happy that he has Michelle in his life, and that she has him to love and adore her as his wife. He is a wonderful step-father and step-grandfather, and his life is full of all the things that he and Michelle share together. We are very happy for them, and our family enjoys any chance we get to be with them. We wish them every blessing in the years ahead.

The fact that together as a family we have made it to the tenth year mark seems unreal. But I can agree with the woman who had said that it takes ten years to turn the corner on grief. It does, and it did, at least in my case. As I write this it has actually been over eleven years since that fateful night when my world and my life were shattered. But I can say that God has helped me to glue the pieces back together again, and there is much to be thankful for and happy about. Do I still miss my Angela? Every single day, I do. Can I find joy and peace in my life now? Absolutely I can, and I always will. And for that I will be forever grateful to my God, and my Savior. I am whole again. Grief did not win in my life or in the lives of anyone in my family. We are better, and stronger, and closer because of the loss we have shared together. And that togetherness will be carried with us all into eternity. And then, once there, we will be reunited with Angela. What a day that will be!

CHAPTER 12

Angela

In this book I have attempted to write about my love for, and loss of my daughter, Angela. I have written about who she was as a little girl, the first child in our family to fill my heart with inexpressible joy. I have shared how she welcomed each of her siblings as they were added, one by one, and how she grew through the process of our family growing. I have mentioned a little bit about her as an adult and what she was doing just prior to leaving this earth. But I have really only scratched the surface of sharing about her as a person.

Angela was independent enough to follow her own dreams and become the very best version of herself without letting others stand in her way. I am sure she did care what other people thought of her, but if their thinking made her feel that she had to change to please them, she resisted and held her ground. She was self-determined in her goal setting, and she had the amazing ability to help others set personal goals for themselves, encouraging them along the way as they stretched to reach those goals. She was a caring and outstanding teacher, a loyal and encouraging friend, and a dearly beloved wife, daughter, and sister, not to mention granddaughter, niece, cousin, sister-in-law, and daughter-in-law. She made a huge impact on the lives of everyone who knew her and loved her, and that impact is her legacy.

Angela was the kind of person who thrived when she had multiple irons in the fire. She juggled her Eugene Symphony Orchestra schedule along with her participation in several other prominent orchestras. She gave weekly lessons to her forty-six or so students that became not only a part of her violin studio, but a part of her family. She cared so much about them that she made time to go with them and their parents to music stores when they needed to purchase a new violin or bow. She often times took violin lessons for her own self-improvement. She never stopped learning and eagerly passed on to her own students the musical skills she was perfecting in herself as she adjusted each skill to her student's developmental level.

As a young college student her desire had been to become the best violinist she could be. To hold her own as she performed with an orchestra was her goal from the outset. As a college graduate, free to explore the world of professional musicianship, she worked very hard to earn her way into many orchestras, and once hired, she gave them the utmost of her integrity and dedication. She enjoyed soloing, but her real cup of tea was being a crucial part of the team, adding to the beauty of the music in her own way, yet at the same time blending into the ensemble perfectly. Even there in the world of symphonic music, she exhibited her leadership skills as she took on roles from section leader to concertmaster, depending on the orchestra. She loved to lead but she excelled most at bringing others alongside herself as she encouraged them to be their very best. Whether she loved music more than she loved people would be difficult to ascertain. But for certain the combination ranked high on her list of her most favorite things.

Those of us who knew her well also knew that she was a multifaceted person. She loved her family first and foremost and was devoted to her husband and the rest of her family above all else. She also loved all kinds of music, her friends, her students, the puppies she and Erik had, and she loved shoes! I added the last one because she managed to use shoes as a way of expressing herself in a world where her working wardrobe consisted of wearing only black, the performance color of choice for musicians. Shoes were such a part of her personality that following her death the women in the orchestra she belonged to wore their prettiest and highest heels in her honor at their first concert without her. We even placed a dozen or so pairs of her heels on the stage for one of her memorial services as a way of depicting a little bit of her spunk and beauty.

Angela had a way of transforming the people around her. It didn't matter if you had known her for just a day or a lifetime, when you parted she had a way of making you feel like you were the only person that mattered to her. A gentleman shared with us in his sympathy card, that he had only met Angela as they participated together for a one time concert with the Oregon Symphony. She was a sub, and they had sat together on a bus ride to the concert hall. It was a little bit of a ride, and she had chatted cheerfully with him as she sat knitting throughout the duration of the trip. She loved to knit winter caps and made dozens of them. Following the concert weekend, the man received in the mail, to his great surprise, the very cap she had been working on as they were getting acquainted. She had such respect for fellow musicians and just had a way of caring about everyone she met that for her to take the time and energy to mail the cap on to another person was just her way of encouraging them. He said he would remember her always and keep the cap that long too.

Among her other attributes, Angela was a salesperson. She sold happiness and joy, and the sheer thrill of living life, by doing what she loved to do most of all. She sold it to her students as she taught them to love music and work hard as they perfected their craft as violinists. She sold it as she shared her life, her home, and even her clothes with some of the young ladies needing "the perfect outfit" for some special event in their life. She sold the idealistic attitude of always doing your best as she led the second violin section of the Eugene Symphony Orchestra. Her encouragement, her going the extra mile to know each person in her section, and her never-ending container of homemade cookies and snacks that she brought to each rehearsal to share became her trademark.

Selling is really nothing more than encouraging someone to invest in something you have to offer them in order to enhance their life in one way or another. Angela combined her love of selling with her passion and love of always being at your best. This served her well when she became a salesperson for a well-known beauty product company. She so enjoyed helping women feel confident and beautiful that she kept her purse, her car, and her home stocked with product, and she found opportunities in life perfect for introducing that product to others. She was known to watch a coveted pair of shoes in a store until they were on sale, and then as she went to purchase them, she managed to engage the salesperson in such a way as to interest her in a particular beauty product. The end result would be that both women made a sale, and Angela's shoes went home with her at a much discounted price thanks to her sale of make-up. She was always ready to help whether it was in the supermarket, the homes of her friends or at her "gigs" with the orchestras where she played. She was not so interested in making a profit as she was in making the world a more confident place, one person at a time. She once told me that when she prepared for a summer concert festival she had to minimize her own luggage in order to have enough room in her car for the beauty products she took with her. She had fun giving free make-overs to anyone who would ask for one. She fully believed that beauty on the inside was better reflected through a confident outside, and so, she endeavored to help everyone else believe that, too. Even men would make purchases for their wives and daughters saying it made a wonderful gift following their absence from home. She loved helping people find the perfect product they were looking for. Upon getting back home her make-up cases would be empty and she would just reorder, and start all over again ready to help whoever would call upon her for more of their favorite products. She loved how selling her products created another way of connecting with people who were friends and perfect strangers alike. No doubt her many customers miss her greatly. Hopefully some have continued on in her campaign of building up the self-esteem of others by the mere use of a mirror!

Angela was 100% the person that she was, which may seem like a crazy statement to make about anyone, but what I mean is that Angela was not pretentious. She did not try to be someone she wasn't, and she didn't want you to be like that either. Her relationships were as authentic as she was. Her faith was very personal to her, and she kept that part of her life fairly private. Angela did not want to push her faith onto anyone, but she also did not want to accept her faith from anyone, except God alone.

When Angela was very young I was the children's choir director at the church where my husband was the minister of music. I oversaw a choir of about one hundred first and second graders, and we performed a children's musical at Christmas, and another one around Mother's Day. Because I was organizing the programs and directing them, I had to spend a lot of time learning the music myself. As a result, our own children were quite used to hearing the musicals played at home. Angela especially enjoyed them and would recite the narrative between songs, and then sing along with great gusto. The Christmas musical we were practicing the fall she was three and a half years old was one she especially enjoyed. It was the retelling of the Christmas story from the stable animals' point of view. The animals talked about how Jesus, God's Son, had been born in their stable. They share that God's plan for Jesus included his growing up, his sacrificial death on the cross, and his resurrection from the tomb three days later. It was a very inclusive children's Christmas musical filled with Biblical truth. I spent most of the summer learning each song and the narration as I prepared to begin rehearsals later that fall with my children's choir.

One particular narrative peaked Angela's interest more than any other, and that was the short narrative about Jesus being nailed to the cross to die for our sins. The lambs in the stable had been speaking about how Jesus was the perfect sacrificial lamb, and that there would be no need for any other. Angela listened intently to this part of the story and kept asking me why they put screws in Jesus' hands and feet on the cross. I really felt she was too young to be visualizing this, so I usually just stated that Jesus died for our sins, but then I refocused her to the resurrection, and the wonder, and joy of that part of the story. She wasn't side-tracked at all and continued to ask about "the screws" that were in Jesus' hands. Weeks went by with her asking about this, and I began to fast forward this part of the story when I was listening to the musical. Then one day, she came skipping into the kitchen in her usual enthusiastic way and announced, "I know why they used screws to put Jesus on the cross." Wondering if she would ever get past this part of the story, I finally asked her, "Why did they use screws, Angela?" And she responded emphatically, "Because they screwsified him!" With that she giggled and skipped out of the kitchen, leaving me completely stunned. I was not sure if she was trying to be funny or if her love of language and use of big words had just made this connection in her little red-haired head. Nonetheless, I was sure that God understood and probably chuckled at her innocent observation.

Amazingly enough, God used this same musical to bring Angela into a personal relationship with him. Just a few weeks after her revelation about Jesus on the cross, she came to Gordon and me one evening, and in a very determined and serious tone she told us that she wanted to ask Jesus into her heart. To say that we were unprepared for this would be an understatement. Neither of us had considered that such an important spiritual decision should or could be made at such an early age. But we trusted God as did Angela, and that night she prayed and asked Jesus to forgive her of her sins, and to be her Savior. Gordon and I tucked the event deep down into our hearts, and I marked the date in my Bible.

Two years later as a kindergartner, Angela came home from

school, and told me that she knew some of her friends at school did not know Jesus. I wondered what she was saying to them to come to this conclusion. As I inquired further, she just sighed and said, "When I pray at lunchtime, some of the children laugh at me." I realized we had never taught her how to pray silently. She learned about silent prayer that night at the dinner table, and then the laughing at school stopped. Angela took her faith in God, and relationship with Jesus, very seriously. So much so that one evening while Gordon and I were out of town, and she and Josh were at a friend's house, Angela prayed with her then, three year old brother, and led him to a personal faith in Jesus. She was only five, yet knowing that her brother had accepted Christ, and was ready for heaven because of it, was of upmost importance to her. I marked the date in my Bible, and thanked God for a daughter with a heart so tender.

As a high school student Angela went on two separate mission trips with her youth group to Mexico. Her love of language had led her to take Spanish class at school every year and that had enabled her to become fluent in Spanish. Because of this, she was asked to be one of two interpreters on the mission trip. God touched her heart for others as she interpreted for those leading the Vacation Bible School program for the children and their parents in that little remote village in Mexico. Angela had the opportunity to help lead many to a saving faith in Christ during those two mission trips. The experience changed her life and her priorities after living amongst those who had so very little by way of worldly possessions, and yet were so happy to possess the truth of God's love for themselves.

As an adult, I have no doubt that Angela's attitude of giving to others and enjoyment in the many relationships she had with her students, co-musicians, friends, and family came out of a heart filled with the love that God had given her throughout her life. His love permeated her life, and poured out on everyone she knew.

Shortly after her death, Erik, her husband, found a recent Bible study that Angela had been using. It was a study on the Gospel of

John. Erik allowed Gordon and me to take the study guide home and read through it. As I read Angela's handwritten answers to the questions asked in each chapter, the insight I saw not only into Angela's walk with God but his providential hand on her life captured my heart. I copied down some of her notations, and I refer to them often as a part of my devotional time when her birthday comes around as well as on the date of her passing. Angela's thoughts as she read through this study about God becoming man in the person of Jesus Christ are personal, of course, and very specific to the place she was in spiritually in her life. Her words have been comfort and balm to my aching heart, and they have also been conclusive evidence of her faith, and of her being nestled safely in her heavenly home with the God who loved her so very much.

One particular lesson was about the blind man that Jesus healed. The scripture used is from John 9:1-3, and it says, "As he (Jesus) went along, he saw a man blind from birth. His disciples asked him, 'Rabbi, who sinned, this man or his parents, that he was born blind?' 'Neither this man nor his parents sinned,' said Jesus, 'but this happened so that the work of God might be displayed in his life.' " The story continues on and ends with Jesus healing the blind man. The study questions began by being focused on the blind man, the spectators that were there, and on Jesus, and how he chose to restore sight to this man. One question asks the reader to contemplate their own imperfections and weaknesses, and asks how God can use them for his glory? When asked about how God could use her weaknesses or problems for his glory and purposes, Angela wrote "I have no value in and of myself, only to others, and in my purpose in life, which is given by God. In God, and his purpose for me, I am invaluable. In him, I am of immeasurable worth, and am effective. In him I am perfected. With him I can accomplish my full potential, in perfect time, and to the greatest effect. This is my self-worth and value." Another question asked why God would choose to use our weaknesses in the first place. Angela answered, "Because it is undeniably not of us! Our lessons are taught to us over the course of our whole lives, and for a large part are built into us, like the blind man's blindness. The lessons make us stronger, and improve us. It's a journey!" The question that grabbed me the most, and still does to this day, asked about the insight she had learned from the passage pertaining to the struggles of life, to which Angela answered, "Sometimes what we go through is for us, sometimes it's a lesson for others, and sometimes it's only to show that God is alive and working."

Angela's answers have humbled me and encouraged me as I have tucked them into my heart. I find her thoughts compelling and providential, as it was only a short amount of time, comparatively, from the moments she took to write them down to the moment she met God face to face. I know God is alive and working, and for me to know that Angela believed that to be true in her life as well is worth more to me than anything else.

Angela certainly was an amazingly gifted musician but more importantly, she was an amazingly gifted human being. She derived purpose and resolve in sharing every single gift God bestowed upon her to those around her, no matter their station in life, their own giftedness or lack of it, or their relationship to her. At her memorial service her husband, Erik, stated that she was the kindest person he had ever known. Her kindnesses came from her heart's purpose of not missing a single opportunity to touch another person's life for good. And that came from her view of herself in God's eyes and his purpose for her. Would that we could all see ourselves that way!

As I close this chapter, I hope I have enabled you to know a little about the Angela that I knew and loved so very much. I also hope that you have come to see the God who created her is the same God that oversaw her life right up to the time of her death. I believe with all my heart that he held her close as she entered heaven and began her immortal life there, never to face fear or pain or death again. And I know that as I have faced the loss of Angela, that same God has carried me forward, day by day, giving me peace and comfort as I continue to live my life without her.

I can't express in words how excited I am to hug Angela again someday. I can't wait to tell her how she has impacted and influenced my life. I believe I know why eternity is never-ending, because it will take me that long to share everything I long to share with her. In the meantime, as I think of Angela I will continue to shed tears but I will also smile and laugh as I remember her. For I know a bit of her lingers and lives on in my heart, as well as in the hearts of everyone she knew and loved. Angela was indeed God's Joyous Messenger to me, and I will always be grateful for God's gifting of her in my life.

CHAPTER 13
Beginnings and Endings

It seems to me that as human beings, we don't often think about the end of a season of our life or the close of a chapter when we are at the beginning of it. When Gordon and I brought each of our newborn children home from the hospital the last thing we were thinking about was the day they would pack up all their belongings as they headed off to college or another opportunity following their high school graduation. It just wasn't on our radar back then. But eventually they all grew up and left home to start life on their own terms. And I am sure like most couples when Gordon and I stood toe-to-toe and took our marriage vows, even though we said words like "for better or worse, in sickness and in health, for richer or poorer, until death do we part" neither one of us was focusing on the fact that one day we might be standing at the graveside of the other. I am certain neither of my parents thought about that on their wedding day either, but it is what happened for them, and one day, it will likely happen for one of us.

Life is all about new beginnings, and yet each one comes with an ending to the story. When you take a new job and experience your first day there, time will indeed bring you to your last day at that same work place. It doesn't matter whether the circumstance stems from a promotion, being fired or retiring after spending decades of successful employment, eventually that job will end. People move

into new towns and put down roots, only to move away again someday and begin life in a new location. Friends are made and enjoyed,
and then are left behind for new friends and new experiences in the
days ahead. Businesses begin and businesses close, sometimes all too
soon from beginning to end.

All of life is a cycle of starts and finishes, and beginnings and
endings, and yet for some reason the endings often times come as
surprises to us. Even situations that we do plan from start to finish
take unexpected turns. A couple wanting a child are thrilled with
the news of their pregnancy and hope with great expectation for the
end result to be that of a healthy baby. Young lovers plan their perfect
lives together assuming they will spend their golden days in marriage
sitting together on their porch with decades of memories filling their
picture albums and their hearts. Students work diligently for years
to become prepared for their chosen vocation, planning every detail
of their successful career. We work, we plan, we prepare, we hope,
we dream, and we follow through the scenario of our lives with the
surety that all will go as planned. But life doesn't work that way
very often. Sometimes pregnancies end in disappointment, babies
are born with challenges, marriages end in divorce, and careers often times take detours we never saw coming. All in all, the endings
connected to the beginnings in our lives can shock us to the core,
and even discourage us from wanting to start over again.

I have found that the one and only thing I can count on not
ending in my life, aside from God's presence, believe it or not, is
my life itself. My life began when I was conceived by the love of my
parents, and the grace of God, and it is by that grace that I know
for certain that my life will never end. It will continue to change,
and I will most likely be caught off guard by circumstances and life
events until the day I die. But the day that I do die and leave this
earth, I will only be experiencing the end of living in one place and
the beginning of living in another. Death will come to my body, but

it will not come to my soul. I have a loving and omnipotent God to thank for that.

Because God is who he says he is, and because he has accomplished his plan of salvation through the death and resurrection of Jesus Christ his Son, I can rest in his assurance that eternity for me will involve being with him in heaven, and also being with everyone else who has trusted him for the same. That includes my family, and nothing matters more to me than that fact.

That may seem presumptuous, but I base my faith on the knowledge I have found in God's Word and by the experience of God in my life. Losing Angela, my daughter, brought me to an ending in my life that I never ever wanted to experience. No loving parent ever wants to outlive their child. It just isn't natural and is almost unbearable. But it happens, and it happened to me. I died a little, as I stated earlier, when my father died. And I died a little more when my mother died. But when my daughter died, it felt like my inner self died completely. My body attempted to keep on going, but inside everything came to a screeching, grinding halt.

Grief has a beginning, but it can be one of those rare things in life that really has no ending. Like life itself, it just changes with time. You never get over it, you just have to get through it, but even then, in some form or another, it can stay with you. But there will come a day when grief will end for those who put their faith in Jesus Christ and their trust in God. The sting of death, and the agonizing grief it brings, will be no more, and what remains promises to be radiant life filled with inexpressible joy and hope fulfilled...beyond our dreams.

My hope is that by writing about the love and loss of my daughter, Angela, and the grief that I have experienced in my lifetime, someone will be encouraged to believe that they, too, can and will make it through the grief in which they are living. Grief does not have to stop us from living, and it certainly does not have to stop us from loving. In fact, it can cause us to live and love at a higher capacity than we ever have before. Grief can be a tool that strengthens us and enables us to be filled with empathy and compassion beyond our means. It can connect us to other human beings in such a way that we can become influencers for good, offering hope in places of the heart where there is none. Those who have been touched by grief can reach out and touch others, making a difference when nothing else will. It is my desire that if you find yourself wrapped in grief, and it feels like there is no end, that you will believe there is a new beginning coming for you. God is capable of carrying anyone through the grief that presumes to defeat them. I know this because he has carried me through mine. I pray that you will allow him to carry you through yours.

CHAPTER 14

The Hopeful Side of Grief

A dear, caring friend of mine asked me some questions I have pondered in light of what I have experienced in losing Angela. I have found them to be helpful as I think about moving forward in my life, and as I attempt to bring this book to a close.

One of her questions had to do with sharing my perspective on where I was in my life before losing Angela and where I am today. Perhaps she meant, "Who I was and who I have become." As I think about the journey I have been on these past years since the police officers entered our home and told my husband and me that Angela had been killed, it is difficult to explain how I have gotten from there to here, and how I have changed as a person because of it all.

I am not the same person I was back then. I am stronger in some ways, and, curiously enough, weaker in other ways. The tears, and the emotion that summon them to appear, are never far below the surface of my being. And though I don't cry much when I am alone anymore, tears still well up when I am speaking to someone about what has happened. I wonder if that will ever change. I see it as a weakness, but I think God uses the tears as strength. He has given me more compassion for others who are suffering, and I am able to empathize with their loss more completely than I did before. That is a good thing.

I wish I could say that I don't feel panic in an emergency

anymore, because I would love to be the kind of person who gathers calmness around herself in such situations, but alas, I feel panic. I tend to think fast and act accordingly, and though I usually end up doing the right thing, I tend to do so in a panic. That is never very comforting for those I may be trying to help. Unfortunately, because of the example in my life of emergency situations usually being quite serious, it is hard for me to approach them with an attitude of calmness and an expectation of things working out just fine. It is something I am working on.

Another change I recognize is that grief has had a tendency to continually drain energy from me both physically and emotionally, and because of that I am more aware of my limitations in those areas now than I ever was before all this happened. I have learned to say no to some opportunities that I would have taken on before. That is something I have had to work on throughout my whole life. But saying no and being satisfied with that answer has surely been easier to do the past few years. I find that I have to pace myself when I know I have a day that will demand a lot of energy or one that includes a task I haven't done for a long while. I have always been a person with a great deal of energy and would wake up each morning with my battery fully charged for the day ahead. That energy usually lasted late into the night if need be, and then the next morning I was charged up again, ready for a new day and whatever lay ahead of me. Now, I feel that even if I do begin the day fully charged, I am way past half empty by noon and totally empty by dinner time. Maybe that is due in part to being older, but I think long years of grieving does take a toll on one's capacity to remain energized and focused. I have learned the benefit of giving myself a great deal of grace in this area and have been pleasantly surprised when down times enable me to have a greater reserve for all that life holds for me now.

My husband and I both agree that we feel a great deal older than we probably really are. We are surprised at how tired we get after a normal work day or an especially long week. Perhaps this would be happening to us at our age even if we hadn't lost our daughter, but I tend to think the fatigue factor has been fast-forwarded because of our loss. Maybe that will change and improve as even more time goes by, but maybe not. We have learned we have to take some things in stride and not let our reserved involvement feel like defeat. It hasn't been a bad thing for us to learn how to do.

My good friend asked me something that has really caused me to do some deep thinking. She asked me if there was anything I would have done differently as I review the last years from my present perspective. Connected to that question was the inquiry as to how my experience of loss was any different than I might have expected it to be. I have found these two questions to be very thought-provoking.

As far as doing anything differently, I certainly do have regrets. Most of them involve my family, the people I love most in this world. I regret that during the early months and even years of having lost Angela that I was incapable of reaching outside of myself and my own grief to support my family members in their grief. Much of the time I felt so shrouded in my own experience that it didn't occur to me to be asking questions or spending extra time with each family member to see how they were doing or how they were processing grief in their own way. I regret that greatly.

One analogy that comes to mind is what it would have been like if my family and I had been tossed off the bow of a ship caught in a terrible storm. Of course we would have wanted to find each other and rescue one other from the tempest that threatened to take us over. But if we were struggling so much that keeping our own heads above water was all we could do, we unfortunately wouldn't have been able to rescue anyone else until we were stabilized enough ourselves to bring them to safety. That is what it was like for me. This may sound very self-serving and selfish to you, but my grief was so huge I struggled a great deal of the time to see anything or anyone else in my life. That unfortunately included the people I cared the most about that were also hurting and were in need of loving support.

Curiously enough, I did not experience this same kind of introspectiveness when my parents passed away. I had the immediate responsibility of caring for my younger siblings back then. Being with them and continuing our lifestyle enabled me to focus on them, instead of myself, and to keep me moving forward. I realize that I was doing so in a somewhat numbed way personally, but I didn't know what else to do. I think when Angela died, "layered grief" affected me like the last straw, so to speak, in my life with past griefs, and it brought me to a stage of brokenness that I struggled to recover from for some time. And at the time that Angela was killed, the rest of my children were grown adults. They did not need me the same way my siblings had so many years before. Still, I truly do regret not being there for my family more. I am grateful that they do not seem to hold it against me. If I could do it over again, that is the one thing I would change.

As for how the loss of Angela was different than I would have expected it to be, I can only say it was even more horrible and painful then I had ever imagined it could be. And perhaps unlike a great many parents, I had imagined the scenario a zillion times as I raised my children. Having lost my parents at such a young age, and so close together, the finality of earthy death was always in the back of my mind as I raised my family. It overshadowed my caring for my precious kids constantly. I loved watching my children grow and learn new things as each stage of childhood revealed their giftedness and their independence. But, for example, I also worried about them as I sent them off to school each day and thoroughly enjoyed the days at home when they didn't have to go. When they were ill, I had to push back thoughts of things being worse than they really were. I tried to be excited when they got old enough to participate in week-long church or music camps, but a feeling of uneasiness was just under the surface for me until they returned home. I sweated bullets when they got their driver's licenses, and even more so when they were ready to head out and begin their lives beyond our home-front. I was about as over-protective as you could get as a mom, but thankfully, God gave me a confident and non-fearful husband in Gordon, and he helped balance out my fearfulness. Our children were resilient, and I thank God for that and for his protection over them in the face of my fears and worries. I am so very proud of each one of them and of the kind of adults they have become. They have overcome their own challenges in spite of mine, and have trusted God in that process. They have been tremendous examples to me, and I am so thankful for their love and forgiveness and for their acceptance of me with all my faults.

There is one bit of advice I would like to give to someone else who is grieving a loss, and that is to try and give yourself the time you need to heal. That is different for each person, and it totally depends on the type of loss you have experienced. But consistent in each situation should be the ability to lower expectations you may have for yourself or for others in your family as you grow through your grief. Do not let anyone place any expectations of healing, in any specific way or any specific timeline, upon you. No one can live through your grief the same way that you will. That is not to say that support and assistance from a qualified grief counselor isn't worth its weight in gold. I would have given anything if my siblings and I had been offered such assistance in our time of need. And the help my family and I received from such persons after losing Angela was a great benefit to us. But just keep in mind no one can set out a path of healing ahead of you. But they can walk beside you and help you get your footing as you go along.

My husband and family were all so encouraging and supportive of me as I grieved. I recall specific conversations with each one of them that caused me to get some balance as I stumbled along, not knowing exactly what would help lessen the pain I was feeling. But God was truly the closest person to me throughout my grief journey, and if you were to ask me why, I would have to say because he knows me best.

I have tried to express in every chapter of this book how God has gone before me in my life, and how he has walked with me each and every single day. Nothing that has happened has been a surprise to him. Nor has anything been out of his control or purpose for my life. I fully believe that if God is God of all, then he is also God over all. He has proven it over and over again to me.

I cannot give you faith in God. And I am not attempting to do that in this book, but I can tell you that my faith in God has been strengthened and personalized as he has carried me through the loss of Angela and through every other loss in my life as well. God is a person, and he has the capacity to meet me right where I am, and that is exactly what he has done for me. He did not rush me as I grieved, but he cared too much for me to let me get stuck somewhere along the way. So he nudged me along allowing me to sit in his lap with questions and frustrations, and every other imaginable human expression, as I grew through my grief. He enabled me to let go of Angela, in time, and allowed me to see her safely tucked in heaven enjoying the unimaginable peace and love that is also waiting for me one day.

Because of this I do not feel fear about dying. Like everyone else, I don't relish enduring pain when death comes, and I am in no way in any hurry to push for it to happen any time soon. But I do have a longing for heaven, and I look forward to being in God's presence and thanking him for the many blessings he has given me in my lifetime. I can't wait to tell Jesus how grateful I am for his love and sacrifice for me, for Angela, and for everyone else I care so very much about. How awesome it will be to meet the Holy Spirit who has been willing to live within my frail human self and guide me through the darkness of life, enabling me to see light where there was none. And I have already shared with you the unspeakable joy that I look forward to experiencing when I get to embrace my Angela once again. It will be just plain heavenly!

I miss Angela more than I can say on paper. But I understand now that my grief in losing her is specifically connected to the importance she was to me. She was so precious to me, and I loved her so completely; therefore, I have grieved completely at the loss of having her in my life. A grief counselor told me that "to grieve deeply for someone is proof that you loved them deeply, and they deeply affected your life." I know that to be true. That being the case, there is one thing that I am reminded of as I think about grieving the loss of a loved one. And that is this: Very few of us lose a loved one without having other loved ones still in our lives. There are people around us that care about us and that we care very much about, and if we aren't careful we can push them away or shut them out of our lives altogether because of our loss. That would be tragic. To fear loving another person because of the pain we have felt when we lost someone we loved so very much would be devastating. Nothing good could come from doing that.

I am so grateful for the special people in my life. My husband continues to be a source of encouragement. We recognize that we could not have made it through losing Angela without each other. Our children and their spouses are such blessings to us, and we love them so dearly. We rejoice in their successes and pray for them as we look forward to many good times together. The precious grandchildren God has given to us bring unspeakable joy and fill our hearts and lives with love and fun. Each family member is a treasure. They are invaluable to me. I thank God daily for placing them in my life. And I ask God to help me focus intentionally on those I still have with me, even as I continue to grieve for those I miss so very much.

If I can encourage you to do anything as you walk through your grief today, it would be to remind you to draw close to the people you love. They are a very special gift to you. Their relationship, even in the midst of your sorrow, can enrich your life and help you as you grow forward in your grief. None of us will ever get over the losses we have experienced in our lives, but every single one of us can get through them, and we can come out on the other side as healthy, loving individuals. I believe that with all my heart, and it is my prayer for you today.

If by chance you have read this story without the experience of losing a child, I hope it is an experience that never comes your way. I hope even more so that you will be able to extend a hug and a hand towards anyone you know who has had to let go of a child in death. Your compassion and empathy may just be the lifeline they desperately need. And, if you have read this book because you have also lost a child, please know I wish I could sit with you and tell you how very sorry I am that you have had to endure such a loss. It is my desire that I have been able to offer some hope that will help you as you move forward, day by day in your life. I feel your pain. I hope you can feel my hug.

In closing, one last word comes to mind, and that word is "change!" Nothing is a bigger part of life, or better definer of life, than change. That is a word that affects us constantly. For a lot of people, change is exciting. It leads to adventure, and it brings great joy, and fun, and makes life worth living. I personally do not like change. I never have and probably never will, and I really don't do change well. Because for me change often times meant adjusting to something I really didn't want to happen. Or it meant I had to go without something or someone I cared a great deal about. Nonetheless, change happens, and it will continue to happen to me, and to you! The hardest part about losing Angela was the change that took place because of her absence in my life. I missed her being there; it is as simple as that. But as time has passed, and as I have grown through my grief and loss of her, I have realized the change that has taken place within me hasn't been easy, but it has been good, and in many ways, it has been necessary.

I have learned the most exciting truth about change, and that is the fact that God is unchanging. Two of my favorite verses are, Malachi 3:6, "I the Lord do not change." And Hebrews 13:8, "Jesus Christ is the same yesterday and today and forever." This is proof to me that no matter what I face in my life, and no matter what changes come, I can rely upon God to be "unchanged" and to stay just as close to me as he always has been. I can know he will steady me and enable me to face each day, each change, and each challenge, and I will survive. Not in my own strength, but in his. This promise carries me into my future and gives me tremendous hope.

With that I say thank you for taking time to read my story about losing my Angela. It was therapeutic for me to write it. I hope it has been helpful, and hopeful, for you to read it. You are in my prayers.

CHAPTER 15
Angela's Poem

At age eleven, my beloved daughter, Angela, wrote the following poem and gave it to me as her Mother's Day gift. At the bottom of the poem she wrote, "Dedicated to my dearest Mother." It came from her very creative and romantic heart, and though it probably isn't poetically correct, it is priceless to me. Never could she have ever known how very prophetic and precious it would become, especially with the passing of time. I close this book with "Rainbows" by Angela Schuster.

Rainbows

On a morning like this
I look to the sky
The grass wet with dew,
Forest smells fill the air.
I love the whole world,
The peacefulness around me,
I cherish forever.
This one special moment
When rainbows appear,
The mist lifts the ground.
The Fairies peep out

To see this one moment
Alone; so they think.
Many a wish has been shed,
Many a tear let free,
Many a person lost,
Many a dream shattered,
Many a broken heart.
Rainbows paint the picture
Of my loveliest dream,
To hold onto forever,
I will cherish forever.

Thank you, God, for Angela. Thank you for her life, her love, and her legacy. Thank you, most of all, for holding her close until I get there to hug her myself. And thank you for rainbows that remind me of Angela, and that I know she is with me always!

Love,
Her Mom

About the Author

Kathy Schuster and her husband, Gordon, live in Central Washington. Together, she and her husband spent twenty-five years in church music ministry in four large churches in Washington State. She directed the children's choirs and also served as Nursery Director, Teen MOPS Coordinator, and Widow's Might Organizer. Currently, Schuster is a homemaker and enjoys traveling with her husband. They love spending time with their grown children and their spouses and especially their four grandchildren.

Printed in the United States
By Bookmasters